MW00785563

From the

Baseball Library

of

Joe Giannatelli

BABE RUTH
P.—Boston Red Sox
151

Cardboard Gems

A Century of Baseball Cards
& Their Stories, 1869–1969

Khyber Oser, Mark Friedland, & Ron Oser

MASTRO AUCTIONS

7900 S. MADISON STREET
BURR RIDGE, IL 60527
630.472.1200   FX.630.472.1201
WWW.MASTROAUCTIONS.COM

© 2006 Mastro Auctions and Mark Friedland
All rights reserved. No portion of this publication may be produced or transmitted in any form by any means, electronic or mechanical, including photocopy, recording, or any information storage retrieval system, without permission in writing from Mastro Auctions, except by a reviewer who may quote brief passages in a critical article or review to be printed in a magazine, newspaper or electronically transmitted on radio or television.

Unless otherwise noted, all photos used in this book were items previously sold in a Mastro Auction and are shown as a function of promoting those and future auctions.

Published by
Mastro Auctions
7900 S. Madison Street
Burr Ridge, IL 60527

ISBN: 978-0-9716097-2-3

Printed in the United States of America

Printed on recycled paper

Book Design by Jeff Marren

This book is dedicated to my parents Joel and Paula Friedland
for always being there and for teaching me that value trumps price;
and to my wife Hunter, my muse, my inspiration, my North Star.

~Mark Friedland~

TABLE OF CONTENTS

COUNTLESS BOOKS HAVE been written on the subject of baseball cards. Some focus on how to collect them, others on how much they're worth. Almost all of these books are geared toward that unique breed known as "the collector"—crazy individuals such as myself who have passionately spent countless hours, and in some cases near-countless dollars, to seek out cardboard rarities.

list—though many of these entries would easily qualify for such a list. Instead, Friedland and the Osers attempted to cover a wide variety of players and card issues in order to simultaneously weave the history of

issues provide additional context to the depth and breadth of cards that were manufactured from 1869 to 1969.

As the premier sports auction house, Mastro Auctions is pleased to join together with PSA, the leading inde-

FOREWORD —
DOUG ALLEN, PRESIDENT
MASTRO AUCTIONS

breed known as "the collector"—crazy individuals such as myself who have passionately spent countless hours, and in some cases near-countless dollars, to seek out cardboard rarities.

This book is intended for a broader audience. It appeals to anyone with an affinity for baseball and a fascination for the long-lasting impact of figures who have stepped within the white lines of ballpark diamonds to transform this game into what we so fondly call America's Pastime. *Cardboard Gems* covers the first 100 years of baseball cards—and, in turn, the first century of professional baseball—by spotlighting many of the hobby's greatest cards, sets and manufacturers.

When Mark Friedland conceived of the project, teamed up with Khyber Oser and Ron Oser to bring it to fruition, and then pitched the book to Mastro Auctions, we were delighted to sign on as publisher. The mission with this book was not to create a "Greatest Cards"

baseball cards and the game itself.

It should come as no surprise that among the 115 different players depicted on the following pages, immortals such as Ty Cobb, Babe Ruth, Joe DiMaggio, Ted Williams, Willie Mays, Mickey Mantle and Hank Aaron are a dominant presence, just as these same icons dominated the record books and headlines during their careers. Mantle alone occupies 10 different cards on these pages, not only on account of his legendary status but also because, unlike many of his predecessors, he played during a period when a multitude of card sets were produced.

There are 118 different issues among the 153 total selections, running the gamut from mainstream staples such as T206 White Border, 1933 Goudey and 1952 Topps to off-the-beaten-path sets like 1903 Breisch-Williams, 1933 Tattoo Orbit and 1954 Wilson Franks. Whether celebrated or obscure, all of these representative

pendent card-grading service, to bring this book to the collecting hobby and to see it reach the hands of mainstream readers who may soon become baseball-card enthusiasts themselves. For those of you who are just being introduced to the world of baseball cards, we have included an introduction to card history and an appendix section about third-party grading. In addition, estimated retail prices are given for each presented card at the end of its description. These prices are based on either collector-grade VG to EX condition (for the rarer and more condition-sensitive issues of the pre-1930s era) or investment-grade NM/MT condition (for the modern issues of the 1930s through 1960s).

I hope beginners and experts alike will enjoy this fine gallery of cards that have helped provide the flavor, shape and form of our great hobby.

PART 1: THE CARDS
Baseball cards extend nearly as far back as the national pastime itself. After the Civil War, baseball transformed from a leisure activity enjoyed by local enthusiasts on makeshift diamonds to a professional sport with organized leagues, paid players on touring teams, permanent ballparks, and avid spectators. Naturally, these 19th-century fanatics, or fans,

known of these mounted team cards featured baseball's first professional team, the 1869 Cincinnati Red Stockings. Between 1886 and 1890, card production experienced a watershed period. Tobacco companies like Goodwin & Co. and Allen & Ginter issued photographic and beautifully lithographed "inserts" as buying incentives inside cigarette packages such as Old Judge and Gypsy Queen. More

before a second surge in output occurred in the early 1910s. This renaissance was spearheaded by the massive conglomerate American Tobacco Trust, which, between 1909 and 1911, manufactured the famous T205 Gold Border and T206 White Border sets, as well as used the guise of its brandname subsidiaries to author Turkey Red Cabinets, Mecca Double Folders, and Hassan Triple Folders. Adult smok-

A Brief History of the Baseball Card Hobby

desired keepsakes of their favorite athletes—Harry Wright, George Wright, Cap Anson, King Kelly, Tim Keefe, and Old Hoss Radbourn. Picture cards were an ideal souvenir, combining this newfangled game with another seismic innovation in American society: photography.

Among the earliest cardboard collectibles were a sequence of advertising pieces for the Peck & Snyder athletic equipment company. The most well-

expensively produced "premiums," which never underwent the perilous product-packaging environment of their counterparts, were made available by mail order with sufficient proof of purchase. The tobacco cards of this late-1880s era laid the groundwork for all baseball sets to come and, today, remain among the most sought-after cards ever created.

Two decades of sporadic, though important, card production ensued

ers were still the primary clientele for baseball cards, but when sports publications like *Sporting Life* and *The Sporting News*, candy firms like American Caramel and Cracker Jack, and even food company General Baking entered the fray, they managed to expand the consumer demographic to baseball enthusiasts of all ages and interests. It was only a matter of time before young fans—those who idolized diamond deities Ty Cobb, Honus

Wagner, Christy Mathewson, and, later, Babe Ruth—became the target market for virtually all baseball cards.

Following another industry-wide lapse in significant sets, this time because of World War I and the Great

formed all of its competitors for the next several years, with sleek photographic designs and, later, artsy illustrated portraits. Then, in 1952, Topps turned the card world on its head with a groundbreaking set of large-sized, eye-catch-

Collecting," compiled his seminal *American Card Catalog* (*ACC*). In it, Burdick classified sports and nonsports sets according to an alphabetical and numerical system that is still prevalent today. Some of baseball's untitled

Major Card Producers	Year(s) of Production
N172 Old Judge	1887-1890
T205 Gold Border	1911
T206 White Border	1909-1911
E90-1 American Caramel	1909
T3 Turkey Red	1911
T202 Hassan Triple Folders	1912
E145 Cracker Jack	1914-1915
Goudey	1933-1936, 1938-1939, 1941
Play Ball	1939-1941
Bowman	1948-1955
Leaf	1949
Topps	1951-Present

American Card Catalog Designations	
C	Canadian Tobacco
D	Bakery
E	"Early" Candy/Caramel
F	Food
H	Advertising
M	Periodicals
N	19th Century Tobacco
R	"Recent" Gum
T	20th Century Tobacco
V	Canadian
W	Strip/Exhibit Cards

Depression, the Goudey Gum Company arrived on the scene in 1933 to change the face of cards. Youngsters adored Goudey's dynamic designs, its star-studded rosters with Ruth, Lou Gehrig, and Jimmie Foxx, and, of course, its sugary sticks of bubble gum. Goudey held sway throughout the 1930s, until rival Gum, Inc. of Philadelphia took the reins with an influential three-year series called Play Ball that lasted from 1939 to 1941. Due to World War II, no major card issues were released for the next seven years, in what would be the last production hiatus amid the long history of card production. In 1948, the Bowman Gum Company brought back baseball cardboard in full force. Bowman outper-

ing, brilliantly colorful cards headlined by #311, Mickey Mantle. Bowman closed up shop shortly thereafter as Topps consolidated its power for the remainder of the time span covered by this book and long afterwards.

PART 2: THE HOBBY

Among the many childhood pastimes that have blossomed into grownup investments—toys, model trains, dolls, and the like—only one has achieved the widest American appeal: baseball cards. Devoted collectors call it simply "the hobby," as if there is no other pursuit worthy of recognition.

The advent of the hobby in a modern sense dates to the 1930s, when Jefferson Burdick, the "Father of Card

issues, and issues with multiple sponsors, have adopted Burdick's designation as their exclusive titles, such as the T205, T206, and T207 sets of the 1909-1912 period. His system, which crops up throughout this book, employs an initial capital letter to describe the genre, followed by numerals that correspond to the chronological order in which Burdick believed the sets to have been produced.

Burdick's unwieldy task made sense of what had been general chaos. He catalogued the card issues that were then known to exist, created general pricing guidelines, and, through his categorization method, was the first person to distinguish many confusingly similar sets from one another.

Two kinds of hobbyists may have benefited most from Burdick's labor of love: set-builders and type collectors. The former aim to assemble the entire gallery of subjects in a given card issue. Some are satisfied with all of the standard-issue cards; others will not rest until they have acquired a "master set" composed of every possible print variation—those errors or anomalies relating to the picture, typescript, or colors on the front or reverse of a card. Type collectors do not concern themselves with perfection of individual sets. Rather, these determined seekers pursue a single card example from every extant set, or at least from a variety of sets. For example, a type collector might assemble one sample from all candy-related issues, with each exemplar chosen based either on its aesthetics, pictured player, team affiliation, or condition. In Burdick's day, type collectors were not uncommon. Today, they are far outnumbered by set-builders who thrill in the chase for that elusive missing number or for that higher-graded replacement card.

Many of the modern hobbyists who took up the mantel of Burdick's legacy and forged a new industry were the children of the post-war baby boom. Too young to read *The American Card Catalog*, these baseball-crazed youngsters clutched pennies and ran to the corner store with two things on their minds: bubble gum and baseball cards. They pointed out a box of packs behind the counter, handed over their hard-earned allowance money, and dashed outside to rip open the card cache in a fit of joy. They were obsessed with the game and its superstars. These were the Golden Years of baseball. Who might surface in this round of pack-opening? A big-time star like Duke Snider, Willie Mays, Jackie Robinson, Ted Williams or Mickey Mantle, or maybe a celebrated local favorite—Richie Ashburn, George Kell, or Nellie Fox. This was a game of chance with a win-win scenario. If the wrong cards came up, the hunt continued tomorrow or next week with a new pack. And no cards went to waste. They were either rubber-banded for safekeeping, traded among friends for different players, "spoked" in bicycle wheels to replicate

the vroom of a motorcycle, or "flipped" in a game to see whose cards could land closest to the base of a wall (as illustrated by the photo on the next spread).

Some stickball players, fan-club members, and bleacher boys of the 1950s grew into the twenty-something collectors of the late 1960s and early 1970s, budding entrepreneurs who frequented baseball-card conventions and viewed cards differently than had their predecessors of the Burdick era. These trailblazers were the first to fully comprehend the investment potential of baseball cards and to actually make a modest living on cards alone. They learned everything they could from the old masters and became experts themselves, memorizing the wisdom of hobby publications like *The Trader Speaks*. They now "flipped" cards in a new way—buying and selling them like day traders on the floor of the New York Stock Exchange. Most significantly, they placed importance and value on condition.

Those same collectors who had dinged, creased, folded, mangled, and destroyed their cards as children—per-

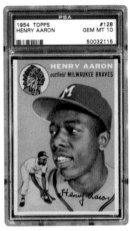

haps because they had done so—now became infatuated with preservation. Drawing from other collecting disciplines, a grading system took hold that ranged from Poor (PR) to Fair (FR) to Good (GD) to Very Good (VG) to

hobbyists strove to own the highest-graded Mickey Mantle 1952 Topps card or the highest-graded 1952 Topps complete set. The upward trend continued throughout the 1990s and into the new millennium, particularly after the

card-convention stalwarts have turned their attention to a new horizon: on-line auctions. The Internet has made cards more accessible to people across the country and around the globe, many of whom were outside the collecting fold

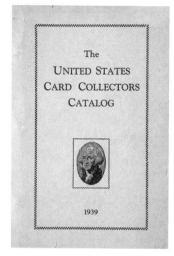  

Three early hobby publications, including, at left, the 1939 first edition of Jefferson Burdick's *American Card Catalog* (originally entitled *The United States Card Collectors Catalog*).

Excellent (EX) to Excellent to Mint (EX/MT) to Near Mint (NM) to Mint (MT), with further combinations of any adjacent tiers such as VG/EX or NM/MT. By the mid-1980s, this new breed of professional collector came to be known as "dealers." Many of them ran card stores during the week and then attended countless shows and conventions on the weekends. Price guides like *Beckett Monthly* were their bibles of the industry.

Soon, there was talk of rising third-party grading services. These companies could be hired to analyze cards down to the micro-fibers, give the cards an official grade, and seal them in Lucite holders. Prices began skyrocketing for star cards and common cards alike as

dot-com bubble burst and investors sought to diversify their financial portfolios with material, tangible collectibles. In July of 2000, a T206 Honus Wagner card newly holdered at the NM-MT 8 level by grading service PSA—the very same card that had been bought a decade earlier in "raw" form by Wayne Gretzky and Bruce McNall for $451,000—sold at auction for $1.26 million. Thanks in large part to third-party grading, baseball cards are fast approaching the prestige of antiques and fine art while showing no signs of losing momentum.

Every day, the hobby expands to include more record-breaking prices and more adherents. In the Digital Age, countless mail-order businesses and

but remember cards from their childhood...and who now yearn to rekindle that nostalgia in adulthood. They are not alone. They are joined by millions more. Just as baseball is our national pastime, baseball cards are our national hobby.

OUR JOURNEY THROUGH a century of baseball cardboard begins with this mounted sepia photograph, sponsored by the sporting goods company Peck & Snyder, that depicts the sport's very breeding ground for baseball. In 1869, a group of Ohio investors sponsored Manager Harry Wright and his Cincinnati nine, making the Red Stockings the first-ever openly paid players. Led by baseball's own version ballclub in this mounted, photographic card. The company's advertisement appears on the reverse, depicting a caricatured ballplayer addled with bats, cleats, belts, and early "lemon peel" baseballs. (Noticeably, he carries no

1869 Peck & Snyder —
Cincinnati Red Stockings

first professional team. Baseball had originated on Hoboken's Elysian Fields in 1845, but the nascent game was pure leisure then—a "hobby," if you will. The teams that sprouted up in New York of the "Wright Brothers"—pioneers Harry and George Wright—the Red Stockings proved a wise investment. The squad went undefeated in 50-some contests, with roughly one-third gloves, because such implements wouldn't enter the landscape of our bare-handed national pastime for several more decades.) On the elegant, studio-format front, Harry Wright,

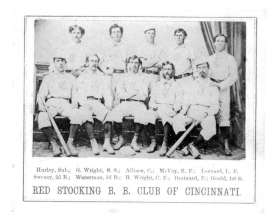

Hurley, Sub.; G. Wright, S. S.; Allison, C.; McVey, R. F.; Leonard, L. F. Sweasy, 2d B.; Waterman, 3d B.; H. Wright, C. F.; Brainard, P.; Gould, 1st B.

RED STOCKING B. B. CLUB OF CINCINNATI.

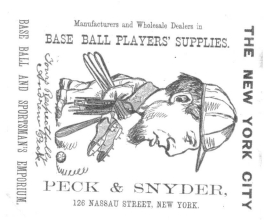

Manufacturers and Wholesale Dealers in
BASE BALL PLAYERS' SUPPLIES.
BASE BALL AND SPORTSMAN'S EMPORIUM.
THE NEW YORK CITY
PECK & SNYDER,
126 NASSAU STREET, NEW YORK.

and New Jersey had aspirations only to enjoy themselves, draw a crowd, and see the American sport grow in popularity. As to the latter, no one foresaw that the biggest factor in baseball's proliferation would be an imminent skirmish known as the U.S. Civil War, when soldiers would teach each other the rules, organize games on makeshift diamonds, and after the war, return to their disparate cities and towns ready to attract adherents. Cincinnati was a of those victories coming in a month-long eastern tour against rivals from Massachusetts all the way to Maryland. Their dominance was highlighted by a game against the New York Mutuals in which the Red Stockings won by a score of 80-5! Asa Brainard starred on the mound that historic season, while George Wright excelled at the plate, reputedly hitting 49 home runs and batting over .600. New York-based Peck & Snyder immortalized the deemed one of baseball's "founding fathers," sits front and center, surrounded by his hirsute colleagues. The image mesmerizes both for its historical importance and period details—the pair of wooden war clubs, the high-topped footwear, the Olde English "C" on the jerseys, and, of course, the signature red stockings.

Estimated Value: $20,000

O THE UNINITIATED EYE, this quoted header might look to be Mickey Welch's nickname, as if the Hall of Fame right-hander was characterized by solemn fair-mindedness and a penchant for long,

Tim Keefe. The issue's relative success fueled the ensuing 1887-1890 sepia release that generally defines the Old Judge legacy, a creation of Biblical proportions that—with its immense roster of 500 players and well over 2,000

graphs by Joseph Wood, whose copyright line appears on each card's advertising reverse. The 1886 Giants were third-place finishers in the National League, and, incredibly, their entire total of 75 wins came from the arms of

1886 N167 Old Judge — Mickey Welch

black robes. But anyone in the know, back in the 1880s or today, would associate Welch with his actual cognomen "Smiling Mickey" and identify "Old Judge" as the cigarette brand that put

different images—has become both the ecstasy and bane of many a set-builder's life. Unsurprisingly, those latter Old Judges of N172 and N173 categorization tend to obscure the hum-

Welch (33) and Keefe (42). Together, the duo logged 118 of the team's 119 complete games—a sharp contrast from the four- and five-game rotations of modern-day, reliever-heavy pitching

baseball cards on the map. Goodwin & Co.'s flagship series began in 1886 with a 12-subject black-and-white set of the manufacturer's hometown New York Giants, including eventual Cooperstown confreres Welch (misspelled "Welsh"), Buck Ewing, Roger Connor, John Ward, Jim O'Rourke, and

ble, yet excessively rare N167s that heralded their arrival. (A comparison could be made to the esoteric interest in Topps' minor offerings of 1951 compared to the outright obsession with its widely revered 1952 production.) Welch and company are pictured in artistic renderings based on photo-

staffs. Welch, who is recognized as the game's first-ever pinch hitter and the only hurler to send his first nine batters down swinging, retired in 1889 as the pastime's third "300 Game Winner," along with Keefe and Pud Galvin.
Estimated Value: $25,000

B EFORE HE FOUND HIS calling in the pulpit, Billy Sunday devoted eight years of his life to the baseball diamond. Ironically, Sunday's greatest strength as a ballplayer was something he would later denounce to his flock—thievery. The fleet-footed outfielder stole bases like a master burglar. In 1891, at the peak of his brief career, Sunday turned his back on a hefty playing salary and took a low-paying administrative job at the Chicago YMCA, explaining, "I heard the Lord ask me to play ball for Him, so I signed up." By the turn of the century, he was a fixture on the gospel circuit, delivering fire-and-brimstone sermons at churches and tent revivals across the land. Upon Sunday's death in 1935, *The New York Times* called him "the greatest high-pressure and mass-conversion Christian evangelist that America has ever known." Imagine the embarrassment and remorse, then, for the producers of 1887's Four Base Hits set, which had mistakenly identified Sunday as his Chicago White Stockings teammate Tom Daly (whose name is even misspelled as "Daily"). One wonders if in such an age of religious fervor, the guilty typesetter later made amends for his transgression at one of Sunday's soul-saving revivals. *Estimated Value: $15,000*

1887 FOUR BASE HITS "DAILY" ERROR — BILLY SUNDAY

ONLY TWO PITCHING records have stood the test of time and will likely prove unassailable: Cy Young's 511 lifetime wins and Charles "Old Hoss" Radbourn's 59 wins in a single season. Radbourn's 59. He then added a trio of postseason complete-game victories in what is considered the first official inter-league championship, 1884's embryonic version of the "World Series." By the time Goodwin & Co. introduced its epic

1887 N172 Old Judge — "Old Hoss" Radbourn

annus mirabilis of 1884 witnessed the Providence Grays workhorse firing 441 strikeouts and going the distance 73 times en route to what was long determined to be 60 conquests, but which statisticians now believe actually totaled 1887-1890 Old Judge insert cards (designated N172) and cabinet cards (N173), Radbourn had joined the ranks of Providence's nearby rival Boston Beaneaters. The future Hall of Famer tallied 309 wins in his eleven professional seasons and, amazingly, completed 488 of the 502 games that he started.

Estimated Value: $4,000

EVERYONE KNOWS Jackie Robinson broke baseball's color barrier, but what about the sound barrier? William Ellsworth Hoy was the first well-known deaf ballplayer. In 14 seasons, the impairment. (New York Giants hurler Dummy Taylor once pitched to Hoy in 1902, marking the only time two deaf players ever faced each other in the majors.) Hoy enjoyed a long, fruitful life after baseball, owning a dairy farm in

1887 N172 Old Judge — Dummy Hoy

slightly built outfielder amassed more than 2,000 hits and almost 600 stolen bases. Had he played in a later generation, Hoy would have gathered a fair share of Golden Glove Awards as well. He corralled any ball that came his way, and once threw out three runners at home plate in a single game. Hoy's nickname "Dummy" seems harsh by today's standards of cultural sensitivity, but it was not uncommon at the time as an immediate indication of hearing Ohio and also working for the Goodyear Tire and Rubber Company. Many fans in the deaf community endorsed him as a candidate for the Hall of Fame...to no avail. Hoy died on December 15, 1961, a mere six months short of turning 100. His full-length Old Judge depiction is characteristic of the prestigious issue in that the photography studio used a pastoral backdrop and then, interestingly enough, suspended a motionless baseball from the ceiling for Hoy's catching pose. Few cards pay tribute to this inspiring figure who never heard the crack of the bat nor roar of the crowd, and who relied on sight, touch, and instinct to hone his skills in the soundless ballpark.

Estimated Value: $2,000

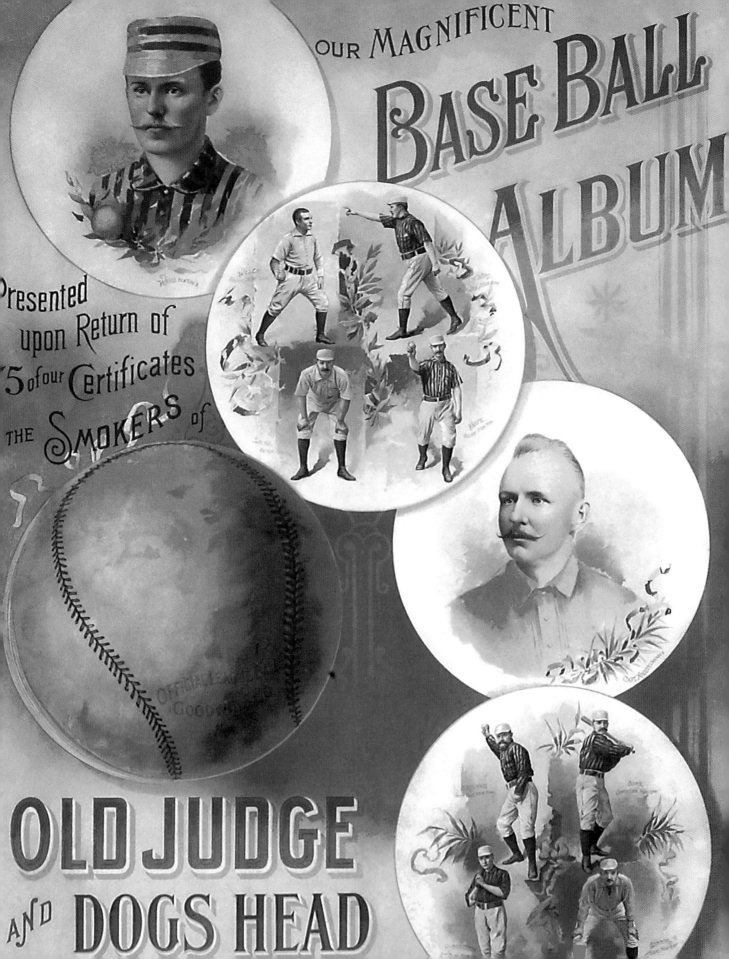

ADRIAN "CAP" ANSON was to the late-nineteenth century what Ty Cobb was to the early-twentieth century. A consummate competitor, Anson was the era's leading batsman and a

Anson occupies several format varieties. He is depicted in uniform and in street clothes on two different small-sized insert cards, then attired in the latter for this larger, cabinet-card premium, available only in exchange for mail-in

1887 N173 Old Judge Cabinets — Cap Anson

model of consistency, as well as a major draw for spectators. He plied his craft for 27 seasons (1871-1897), averaging between .308 and .415 for 20 of those campaigns. At career's end, the 45-year-old first baseman claimed 3,418 career hits— making him the founding member of the "3,000 Hit Club." Even more impressive, Anson had served double duty for the majority of those seasons, managing Chicago's National League team in addition to his playing responsibilities. He was widely held to be among the game's greatest strategists, and is credited with initiating the annual migration ritual known as spring training. In Goodwin & Company's Old Judge production,

coupons. The crystal-clear studio portrait, brilliant of its own accord, is further enhanced by the gold lettering and gilt-lined perimeter of the mount. Issued from 1887 to 1890, Old Judges represent one of the most daunting challenges in the card-collecting sphere. To date, no hobbyist has been able to assemble a "complete" set of the more than 2,000 cards, let alone gather at least one sample from all 500-plus players. Achieving either goal, even without regard for condition, would be tantamount to possessing the Holy Grail of nineteenth-century collectibles.

Estimated Value: $10,000

BEFORE 1887, MIKE KELLY went by the name "King." Henceforth, he was also known as "$10,000 Kelly." The popular right fielder gained renown as much for his charisma and rebellious antics as for

Anson, and Tim Keefe representing the Hall of Fame contingent. After peaking with the White Stockings, Kelly's career went steadily downhill. Even his audacious base-running, to which Anson attributed the origin of the hit-and-run,

1887 N175 LARGE GYPSY QUEEN — KING KELLY

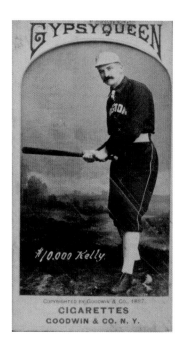

his high level of play or winning ways. In seven seasons with the Chicago White Stockings (1880-1886), he and player/manager Cap Anson led their squad to five first-place finishes. Kelly was at the top of his game in 1886, leading all hitters in average (.388), on-base percentage (.483) and runs (155), while swiping 53 bases. Seizing on his success, the White Stockings sold their enigmatic star to the Boston Beaneaters for a king's ransom in nineteenth-century America: ten grand. Later that year, the newly christened "$10,000 Kelly" made his Boston-uniform debut in Goodwin & Company's Gypsy Queen set. Gypsy Queens were produced in two sizes: the smaller, standard-issue cards and a much scarcer, larger format. Only nine distinct designs are thought to exist in the oversized variety, with Kelly,

had lost its intensity. By 1889, the battle cry "Slide, Kelly, Slide" had become a satirical song of the same name. Frank Harding's lyrics (which allude to the era's globe-trotting journey of all-star players on "Spalding's Australian Base Ball Tour") went, "*Slide, Kelly, Slide! / Your running's a disgrace! / Slide, Kelly, Slide! / Stay there, hold your base! / If some one doesn't steal you, / And your batting doesn't fail you, / They'll take you to Australia! / Slide, Kelly, Slide!*" King Kelly played the next few seasons with Boston, Cincinnati's Kelly's Killers (of the American Association), and the New York Giants. He retired from the game in 1893, died of pneumonia the following year, and was inducted to Cooperstown in 1945.

Estimated Value: $15,000

Mike "King" Kelly (seated center) and the 1887 Boston Base Ball Club.

BOSTON B. B. C.

$\mathcal{A}$H, KALAMAZOO Bats. The nineteenth-century issue with the unforgettably enchanting name is comprised of player and team cards, as well as larger-sized cabinets. Most "Pictures") could be exchanged for prizes according to a conversion table. Each prize had a retail value ranging from 25¢ to $5—the latter a rather hefty amount when adjusting for inflation. Still, anyone who currently owns and boldly printed Kalamazoo Bats legend. Philadelphia Quakers outfielder Jim Fogarty demonstrates an early batting stance, while his crouched teammate Deacon McGuire, who recorded at-bats in 26 seasons between 1884

1887 N690 Kalamazoo Bats — Jim Fogarty/Deacon McGuire

Kalamazoo Bats are blank-backed by design. Encountering one with an advertising reverse is a rare treat indeed, and not solely for the sake of its the grand-prize "silk umbrella" would be wise to accept an in-kind trade for *one* well-chosen card, let alone 400. Take this specimen, for example, which realized and 1912, sports the finest in catcher's equipment—that is to say, none whatsoever. It would be a daunting, if not impossible, task to assemble the checklisted

elusiveness. The terms of redemption offered by manufacturer Chas. Gross & Co. of Philadelphia are downright entertaining. Employed like proof-of-purchase labels, the cards (referred to as almost $3,000 in a 2004 auction, despite being blank-backed and picturing two rather unheralded ballplayers. The card's value rests on its scarcity, charismatic image, clean presentation, set of approximately 60 known N690 cards...unless a hobbyist scoured the earth from Timbuktu to Kalamazoo! *Estimated Value: $2,000*

SCOTTISH-BORN JIM McCormick was one of only 10 ballplayers chosen for this lighthearted edition of caricatures. A usage for advertising, these "trade" cards usually carry the addition of a sponsor's message in the upper-right quadrant—in this case for cigar brand represented relative to non-sports (and often racially provocative) subject matter, but Tobin Lithos and their trade-card kin constitute an extremely sig-

1887 H891 Tobin Lithographs "A Slide For Home" — Jim McCormick

notable contrast to the static studio portraits of many contemporary sets, Tobin Lithographs are beloved for their dazzling colors, artistic quality, and whimsical action scenes. Each rendering conveys a captioned title and surname, along with acknowledgements of team affiliation and manufacturer at the upper-left and lower-right corners, respectively. Because of their intended

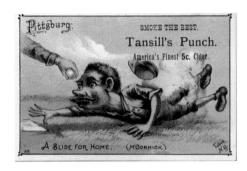

Tansill's Punch. Trade cards of all kinds were an immensely popular phenomenon in the nineteenth century. Baseball themes tend to be surprisingly under-

nificant foundational genre within the baseball-card hobby. McCormick, who dives beneath a fielder's tag in this lively portrayal, was known less as a base runner than as an ace pitcher. In 1880, he led all hurlers with 45 wins, and he retired in 1887 with more than 250 mound victories to his credit. *Estimated Value: $675*

THIS EARLY MINOR-league set was produced by S.F. Hess & Co. of Rochester, New York, yet features 34 ballplayers (and one umpire) from way over yonder on the West Coast. Hobbyists praise the club. He holds a baseball in his right hand and points skyward with his left, indicating either a) he is preparing to throw the ball in unorthodox fashion; b) Godzilla is coming; or c) Hanley is a little teapot, short and stout. S.F. Hess also

1888 N321 S.F. Hess Cal. League — Hanley

40-card issue primarily for its lush lithography and secondarily for its abject scarcity. Mr. Hanley, whose first name remains unknown (as is the case with nearly all of the set's subjects), evidently suited up for the "Haverly's" ball-

released a second, even rarer issue of California Leagues cards that same year—a sepia photographic set designated as N338-1. *Estimated Value: $3,000*

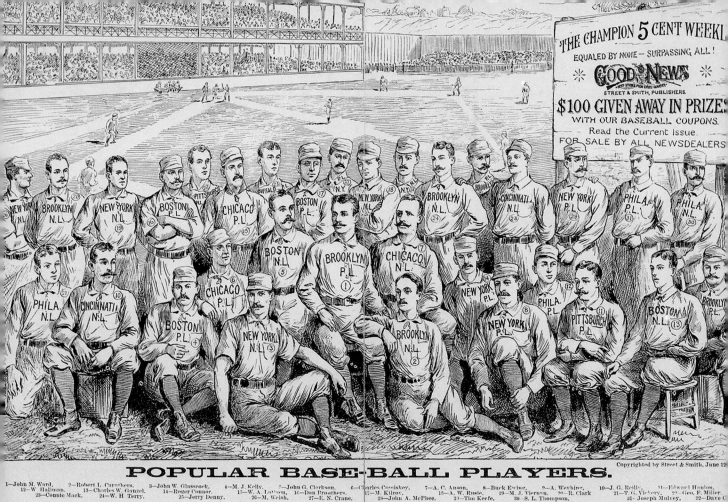

POPULAR BASE-BALL PLAYERS.

Copyrighted by Street & Smith, June 12

1—John M. Ward.   2—Robert L. Caruthers.   3—John W. Glasscock.   4—M. J. Kelly.   5—John G. Clarkson.   6—Charles Comiskey.   7—A. C. Anson.   8—Buck Ewing.   9—A. Weyhing.   10—J. G. Reilly.   11—Edward Hanlon.
12—W. Hallman.   13—Charles W. Ganzel.   14—Roger Connor.   15—W. A. Latham.   16—Dan Brouthers.   17—M. Kilroy.   18—A. W. Rusie.   19—M. J. Tiernan.   20—R. Clark.   21—T. G. Vickery.   22—Geo. F. Miller.
23—Connie Mack.   24—W. H Terry.   25—Jerry Denny.   26—M. Welsh.   27—E. N. Crane.   28—John A. McPhee.   29—Tim Keefe.   30—S. L. Thompson.   31—Joseph Mulvey.   32—Dave C

1888 N403 Yum Yum Tobacco — Tim Keefe

CHICAGO-BASED AUGUST Beck & Co. employed two card designs for its 1888 insert set packaged with Yum Yum-brand tobacco—full-length line drawings of players in action, along with sepia studio portraits that were stylistically similar to other contemporary card issues. New York Giants right-hander Tim Keefe claimed pitching's version of the Triple Crown that year, leading the National League with 35 victories (including a record 19 straight!), 335 strikeouts, and a 1.74 ERA. The mustachioed moundsman, dubbed "Smiling Tim" for reasons unapparent in this prim depiction, came away with 35 wins or more in five different seasons. He also captured three pennants in the 1880s, among them back-to-back titles with the Giants in 1888 and 1889. Despite only 14 major-league campaigns, Keefe posted 342 wins and retired as the game's early record-holder for career strikeouts, with 2,562.

Estimated Value: $10,000

NEW YORK'S

KEEFE, PITCHER,
SMOKE AND CHEW
"YUM YUM" TOBACCO.
A. BECK & CO., CHICAGO, ILL.

THE TEN BALLPLAYERS in Allen & Ginter's 50-card, multi-sport debut included six Hall of Famers: Cap Anson, John Ward, John Clarkson, King Kelly, Tim Keefe, and Charles Comiskey. Comiskey, then (.335). Such on-field achievements of course were not what assured Charlie Comiskey a place in Cooperstown. He was inducted as an "Executive/Pioneer" based on the second phase of his baseball career, when Comiskey co-founded thizers of the so-called Eight Men Out, gave Cicotte, Chick Gandil, Swede Risberg et al. little recourse for fair pay except to "fix" the 1919 World Series. In the end, Commissioner Kenesaw Mountain Landis sentenced the play-

1888 N28 ALLEN & GINTER WORLD'S
CHAMPIONS — CHARLES COMISKEY

the St. Louis Browns' player/manager, was a prime candidate for the issue—and not simply because his candy-cane-striped cap and trimmed lace-up shirt were so well suited for color print-ed the American League in 1901 and then owned the Chicago White Sox for 31 years. Now, one would imagine that because Comiskey had been a player himself, he might have treated his Pale ers to permanent ex-communication from baseball; meanwhile Comiskey, one of the major-league moguls who had actually hired Landis as commis-sioner, shouldered no punishment for

CHARLES COMISKEY.
ALLEN & GINTER'S
Cigarettes.
RICHMOND, VIRGINIA.

ing. The speedy first baseman had steered his squad to a world championship in 1886, the zenith in a string of four consecutive American Association titles. Statistically, Comiskey's finest season coincided with the year of this Allen & Ginter portrait, as he recorded career bests in hits (180), RBI (103), stolen bases (117), and batting average Hose players with the care and respect accorded them. On the contrary, the "Old Roman" was unscrupulous and ruthless, a penny-pinching tyrant who benched 29-game-winner Eddie Cicotte for the final two weeks of the 1919 season to avoid paying the ace a contractually promised 30-win bonus. This and other offenses, allege sympa-his miserly ways—and, perhaps to his delight, wound up minus many of his team's highest salaries. But alas, the "Black Sox Scandal" forever tarnished Comiskey's reputation, in spite of a half-century's ardent devotion to baseball as a player, manager, and executive. *Estimated Value: $1,500*

*L*ONG BEFORE CATCHERS Johnny Bench, Yogi Berra, Roy Campanella, Mickey Cochrane, and Josh Gibson, there was Buck Ewing. Ewing's reputation as the best all-around backstop persisted well

Allen & Ginter's second installment of the "World's Champions" series. The six-card baseball subset is represented in two different formats: 1) a small, portrait-only design that is categorized as N29 and mirrors Allen & Ginter's fore-

1888 N43 ALLEN & GINTER WORLD'S CHAMPIONS — BUCK EWING

after his nineteenth-century career had ended, and, in 1939, he was the first at his position to gain enshrinement at Cooperstown. Donning little if any catcher's gear, Ewing suited up for 18

going effort (N28); and 2) a larger, more elaborately designed edition known as N43 that features the same N29 portraits surrounded by beautiful baseball imagery. Because these exquisite cards

seasons of play with the Troy Trojans, New York Gothams, New York Giants, Cleveland Spiders, and Cincinnati Reds. In the year of this depiction, the Giants captain plied his defensive prowess and solid hitting toward the team's first of two consecutive championships. Ewing is the only Hall of Famer featured in

were originally encased with cigarettes, few examples have avoided rampant staining. If protective wear for catchers was scarce back in Ewing's day, protective sleeves for tobacco inserts were practically non-existent.

Estimated Value: $2,000

AT A TIME WHEN CARD production was still in its infancy, Goodwin & Company showed what was creatively possible. The "Champions" set, distributed in packages of Old Judge and Gypsy Queen tobacco, was a vision of the future, a benchmark for the lithographic excellence in portraiture two decades hence: T205 Gold Borders, T206 White Borders, and, above all, T3 of Famers Cap Anson, Dan Brouthers, Tim Keefe, and King Kelly. Each brilliant rendering conveys the majesty of a royal-court painting or, more appropriately perhaps, a presidential pose. Indeed, one wonders if in the topsy-

1888 N162 Goodwin Champions — Cap Anson

turvy election year of 1888, Anson's esteem among the populace may have rivaled that of lackluster incumbent Benjamin Harrison or resurrected hopeful Grover Cleveland. The White

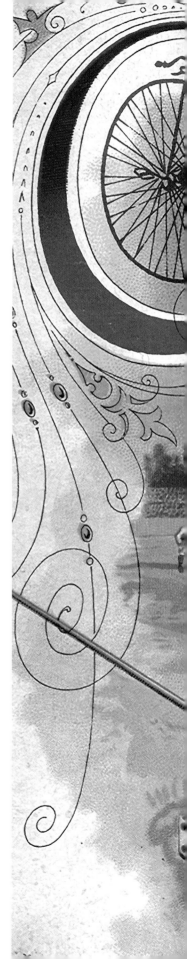

Turkey Reds. The case could be made that nary an issue has surpassed Goodwin's 1888 effort in terms of pure artistry (though the large Turkey Reds do have an inherent advantage over their predecessor in physical size). Eight players comprise the baseball subset of the multi-sport roster, among them Hall

Stocking first baseman's greatness as a batsman, fielder, and tactician, and as a steward of the Grand Old Game, could receive no finer tribute than this nineteenth-century masterpiece, with its signature likeness and Maxfield Parrish-like, glowing sunset.

Estimated Value: $3,000

Jim O'Rourke (seated, far left) with the 1874 Boston Base Ball Club.

G & B WAS AHEAD OF ITS time. The gum company created a baseball set back when cards were still the exclusive domain of tobacco firms. Caramel cards would eventually hit their stride in

Baseball cards were destined to be the profitable passion not of cigarette-smoking adults, but rather their sugar-craving young offspring. Hall of Famer Jim O'Rourke might have had an opinion on the future marketability of cards.

League's Washington Senators with 2,643 lifetime hits and two team championships to his credit. He remained active in baseball as a manager and umpire, and even took the field again as a player at the age of 54, rapping out

1888 E223 G & B Chewing Gum — Jim O'Rourke

the early 1910s, and gum cards did not become pervasive until the 1930s. The avant-garde G & B perhaps understood what the American Tobacco Trust never knew and what Cracker Jack, Goudey, Bowman, and Topps would later learn:

He was, after all, nicknamed "Orator Jim" for his lengthy tracts on a multitude of subjects. O'Rourke began his playing career in 1872 with the Middletown Mansfields of the National Association. In 1893, he retired from the National

one hit in four plate appearances for the New York Giants. O'Rourke's handle-bar mustache adds vintage charm to his E223 portrait, a valuable entry in the first gum-card baseball issue of all time. *Estimated Value: $10,000*

Connie Mack in his later years as a Hall of Fame manager.

AN ORDINARY DECK has 52 playing cards, divided into four suits, each with three royalty face-cards. This baseball-themed deck, on the other hand, numbers 72, contains eight sub-nents, colleagues, and spectators throughout the land. Mack had not yet been crowned when he graced this playing card in 1888. Indeed, the back-stop's early career at the plate— whether catching or batting—was of the National League's eight teams: the New York Giants, Chicago White Stockings, Philadelphia Quakers, Boston Beaneaters, Detroit Wolver-ines, Pittsburgh Alleghenys, Indianapo-lis Hoosiers, and Washington Nationals.

1888 WG1 Base Ball Playing Cards — Connie Mack

sets, and includes only two sovereigns. The first, Mike "King" Kelly, ruled in name alone. The second, Connie Mack, enjoyed his managerial throne for the entire first half of the twentieth centu-ry—the longest reign in baseball histo-ry. His subjects were the Philadelphia Athletics; his admirers were oppo-mediocre at best. Humble beginnings gave way to celebrated ascension, though, as the "Tall Tactician" later man-aged his A's to nine pennants and five championships, while amassing more lifetime wins (3,776) than any other skipper. The 72-card WG1 set depicts one player from every position for each A transfixing tapestry design, of the kind still championed by Bicycle-brand cards today, adorns the reverse. Among the six-dozen subjects, only Mack came to deserve the sobriquet "His Highness," and not solely for his 6-foot-1 frame, but for his majestic legacy.
Estimated Value: $2,000

*P*RODUCED EXCLUSIVELY in Cleveland, "Just So" tobacco cards are ghosts of the hobby. Most collectors will never see an example first hand. One or two copies each of fourteen Cleveland Spiders

er/manager Patsy Tebeau (who would later sign the first American-Indian ballplayer, Louis Sockalexis) plating 102 base runners. Jacob Kitchline Virtue manned first base. In 97 games, Virtue tallied 100 hits and 60 RBI. His

J.K. VIRTUE.

CHEW OR SMOKE **JUST SO**

1893 Just So Tobacco — Jake Virtue

players have been encountered, amounting to about 20 surviving cards. The 1893 Spiders were third-place finishers in the National League, with Cy Young tossing 34 wins, outfielders Jesse Burkett and Buck Ewing batting .348 and .344, respectively, and play-

career spanned 5 years in which almost no card sets were produced—between the tail end of the 1887-1890 Old Judges and the arrival of the 1895 Mayo's Cut Plug release—so his immortality on cardboard was as unlikely as it was fortuitous. Mr. Virtue

appears to have gloried in the photo opportunity, his eyes sparkling and his hair, mustache, and collared uniform arranged...just so.
Estimated Value: $10,000

An illustration of the 1894 Temple Cup Series between the Baltimore Orioles and the New York Giants.

E. J. DELEHANTY, PHILADELPHIA. L. F.

For Chewing and Smoking

POOR ED DELAHANTY. The hard-hitting left fielder hit the bottle too hard one evening midway through the 1903 season. He caused a ruckus on a train from Detroit to New York, was forcibly those of Thurman Munson and Roberto Clemente. All three players had long established their dominion over the sport, and they showed every sign of continuing that success for years to come. Delahanty, who had major-league brothers). Mayo's Cut Plug included the Philadelphia Phillies standout in its sepia-toned 1895 issue—the highlight of an otherwise unspectacular decade for cardboard collectibles. Forty players are pictured

1895 N300 Mayo's Cut Plug — Ed Delahanty

removed by the conductor near the Canadian border, and then either fell, jumped, or was pushed off a bridge into the Niagara River. His body surfaced below Niagara's Horseshoe Falls a week later. Delahanty was 35. His startling death mirrors, to some degree, three times batted over .400 and once went 9-for-9 in a doubleheader, carved a .376 average and 93 RBI in his final full season. He still holds the fourth-best lifetime batting average of .346, which also tops the fraternity of Delahantys (Ed was the eldest of *five* in uniform or in street clothes. That "Big Ed" poses in the latter imbues the card with an eerie twinge, since, finely dressed, he doubtless looked much the same on the night of his mysterious death. *Estimated Value: $3,000*

EVERY JESSE BURKETT card is a cause for celebration, seeing as how the Hall of Famer appeared in so few sets during his 16-year career (1890-1905). Cap Anson's closest rival among nineteenth-century batsmen, Burkett twice fashioned season averages above .400, en route to a lifetime mark of .338 and a grand total of 2,850 safeties. Weekly publication *Sporting Life* featured Burkett in its substantial series of cabinet cards that were produced in several styles between 1902 and 1911. The temperamental outfielder—dubbed "Crab" for reasons made clear by his grim expression—is pictured with the St. Louis Browns, which definitively dates the card to the 1902-1904 period. Jefferson Burdick's *American Card Catalog* classified this release as

1902–1911 W600 SPORTING LIFE CABINETS — JESSE BURKETT

W600, even though the magazine affiliation would appear to necessitate a corresponding "M" rather than the "W" of album and exhibit issues. Distributed inside glassine envelopes, the elegant cabinets were initially available by mail-in redemption and later sold for 10 cents apiece. They are especially prized among modern hobbyists because of photographer Carl Horner's outstanding portraits, some of which were also used for the 1909-11 T206 tobacco series. *Estimated Value: $5,000*

BASEBALL PLAYERS comprise only 14 of the 500-plus athletes, entertainers, and civic leaders in this Herculean undertaking by National Tobacco Works. But hobbyists are not complaining, grateful as they are for the production's striking, oversized sepia portraits of Hall of Famers John Ward and Amos Rusie. Rusie's mounted sepia photograph catches the New York Giants right-hander at a slight turn, dressed in his stylish uniform. The Indiana-born "Hoosier Thunderbolt" had gotten his start at the major-league level in 1889, when he was only 17. By age 27, Rusie had amassed his lifetime

1895 N566 NEWSBOY CABINETS #175 — AMOS RUSIE

total of 245 wins, which included four campaigns of thirty victories or more. Newsboy Cabinets were produced following perhaps his finest season, an 1894 Triple Crown performance of 36 wins, 195 strikeouts, and a 2.78 ERA. In a remarkable passing of the torch, Rusie's career ended soon after the Giants shipped him to the Cincinnati Reds for a young, unknown prospect by the name of Christy Mathewson. *Estimated Value: $3,000*

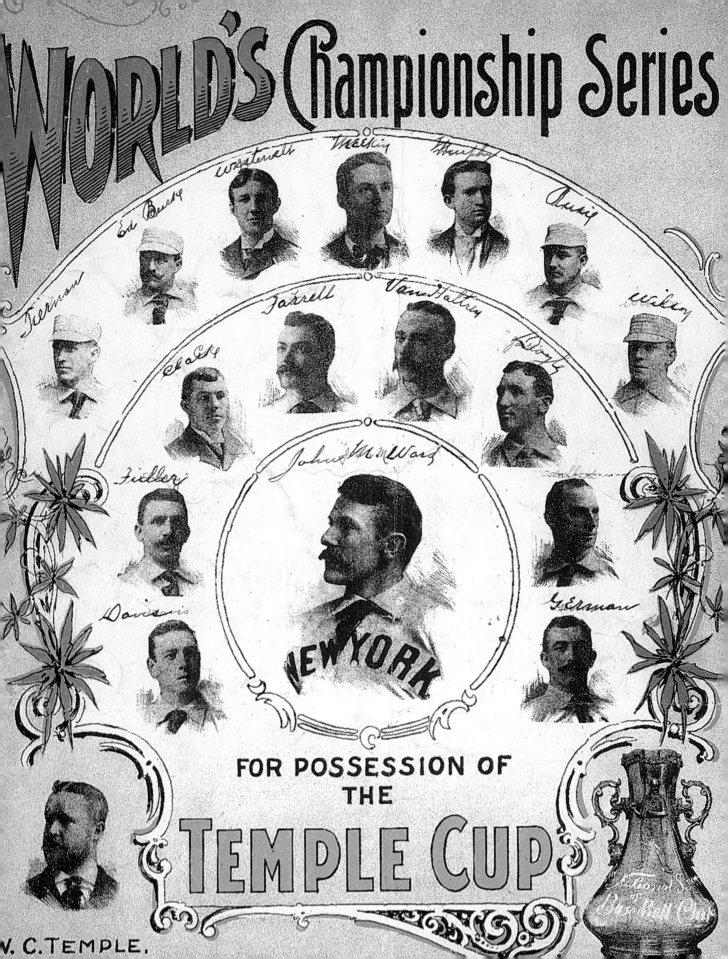

The hand of Cy Young holding the ball from his 500th win.

One of a hundred and fifty prominent Baseball players

YOUNG, P, Boston, A

*D*ENTON TRUE "CY" Young, the winningest pitcher in history and the namesake of his craft's elite annual award, headlines this most significant and early candy-card issue. The the elusive and condition-prohibitive E107s, which boast spellbinding portraits on the front and are either blank-backed or printed with "One of a hundred and fifty prominent Baseball players" on the reverse. In 1903, Cy Young Series, in which Young fired two wins and 17 strikeouts (not to mention drove in 3 runs with his bat) en route to the Boston Pilgrims' 5-games-to-3 triumph over Honus Wagner's Pittsburgh Pirates. Young finally called it quits in

1903 E107 BREISCH-WILLIAMS — CY YOUNG

Breisch-Williams release was one of several sets to fill the noticeable gap between the Old Judge photographic editions of the late 1880s and the American Tobacco Trust's avalanche of illustrated cards beginning in 1909. "E" series enthusiasts bow down before was in his fourteenth of 22 big-league seasons and his third year with Boston. He already had five 30-win campaigns to his credit, and 1903 would yield 28 mound victories, 34 complete games, 7 shutouts, and a 2.08 ERA. The season concluded with the first modern World 1911, though he often showed up at the ballpark for Old-Timers Games. His 511 lifetime conquests outdistances the nearest competitor, Walter Johnson, by nearly 100 and, in all likelihood, will never be overtaken.
Estimated Value: $20,000

S EVERING HIS INDEX FIN-
ger in a childhood accident
never stopped Mordecai
"Three Finger" Brown from achieving
his dream of pitching in the majors.
Indeed, Brown not only broke into the

tially fell victim to their cross-town rival
Chicago White Sox—the famed
"Hitless Wonders"—Brown and company rebounded with back-to-back tri-
umphs over the Detroit Tigers.) That
1906 season also saw Brown surface

ball play—in Mordecai's case, appropriately enough, a "Strike." With his neme-
sis Christy Mathewson conspicuously
absent from the issue, Brown was easily the most celebrated senior-circuit
pitcher in attendance. The pair faced off

1906 WG3 Fan Craze — Mordecai Brown

big leagues, he became one of the
finest hurlers of his generation. Six 20-
win seasons, a lifetime 2.06 ERA, 55
career shutouts, two world championships—these were the hallmarks of
Brown's mound excellence. In 1906,
the Chicago Cubs ace went 26-6 and
averaged a bafflingly low 1.06 runs per
game while leading his team to its first
of three consecutive World Series
appearances. (Although the Cubs ini-

in the Fan Craze card game. Produced
out of Cincinnati, Fan Craze consisted of
a blue-backed release featuring stars of
the recently formed American League,
along with a red-reverse edition showcasing Brown and his fellow National
Leaguers. Both sets of 54 cards were
disseminated in glassine envelopes
and came complete with game board,
playing tokens, instructions, and score-
card. Each portrait bore a specific base-

against each other as many as 25 times
during their concurrent tenures, even
closing out their careers together in a
match-up on September 14, 1916. The
game marked Matty's sole appearance
in any uniform other than the New York
Giants, as the then Cincinnati Reds
manager claimed a 10-8 victory over
Brown's Cubs.
Estimated Value: $250

WITH MASTERFUL portraits by Carl Horner, gilt-embossed circular frames, and lovely surrounding designs, the Rose Company set is in a league of its own among baseball post-

in the N.L. pennant race as the Cubs faced the first-place New York Giants. With the score tied and two outs in the bottom of the ninth, Giants second-sacker Al Bridwell strode to the plate with runners on the corners—Harry

craftily tosses the ball into the stands, thereby disposing of the evidence. Almost immediately, Evers shows up on the second-base bag holding up a ball—perhaps the retrieved original ball, perhaps a substitute. Umpire Hank O'Day

1908–1909 ROSE COMPANY POSTCARDS — JOHNNY EVERS

cards. Each of the approximately 200 cards measures 3-1/2" by 5-1/2", and all of the game's premier players are represented. At the time, Johnny Evers may have been as sought-after a figure

McCormick at third and nineteen-year-old Fred Merkle at first. Bridwell laces a single to center, McCormick crosses home plate for the apparent game-winning run, and Merkle dashes off the

declares Merkle out and then—with the score tied again and Giants manager John McGraw turning irate—calls the game on account of darkness. Two weeks later, Evers and the Cubbies lay

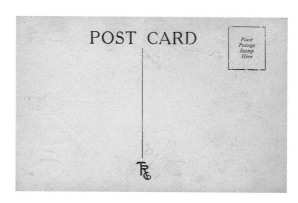

as Ty Cobb, Honus Wagner, or Christy Mathewson. The middleman in the Tinker-Evers-Chance combination won his second straight championship with the Chicago Cubs in 1908. He was also a hero that year in one of the most infamous plays in the annals of baseball: Merkle's Boner. The mishap came late

base path towards his jubilant team-mates...without touching second base. Quick-witted Evers notices Merkle's carelessness and calls for the ball. But the throw from Cubs center fielder Art Hofman overshoots his teammate and winds up near Giants first-base coach Joe "Iron Man" McGinnity, who quite

claim to the gonfalon, advance to the World Series, and repeat as major-league victors in what ultimately will be the last championship in Chicago Cubs franchise history.

Estimated Value: $1,000

Jackson' r.f. Phila. Am.

BASE BALL SERIES
100 SUBJECTS
BASE BALL
CARAMELS
MFG' BY
AMERICAN CARAMEL CO
PHILA., PA.

C ANDY CARDS OFTEN receive short shrift in favor of their more prevalent counterparts packaged with tobacco or gum. Vastly underrepresented in the collecting community, they are an endan-

Jackson by the era's dominant tobacco companies. American Caramel had the inside track. Because the firm was based in Philadelphia, its brain trust of designers knew all about the rural phenom from South Carolina, whose head-

the tobacco consortium may not have overlooked Jackson so much as purposely excluded him. The error of omission paved a road of honor and sweet satisfaction in cardboard candyland, forevermore. Jackson leans on his

1909-1911 E90-1 American Caramel — Joe Jackson

gered species of sorts, and American Caramel's 1909-1911 issue corresponds to the bald eagle—a regal emblem for the cause of preservation. Highlighting the 120-subject cavalcade is Joe Jackson's "true" rookie card, which preceded any formal depiction of

line-grabbing stint with the hometown A's would span two years and a mere 10 games due to Jackson's cold feet (he was "Shoeless Joe," after all) about big-city life. Analyzing the feeble statistics from those 10 appearances in 1908 and 1909, namely 6 hits in 40 at-bats,

Black Betsy bat, lovingly burnished with tobacco juice, against a royal-purple sea—an ideal color for the E90-1 set, "King of the Candy Cards."
Estimated Value: $10,000

Mitchell. r. f. Cincinnati.

BASE BALL SERIES
100 SUBJECTS

BASE BALL
CARAMELS

MFG' BY
AMERICAN CARAMEL CO
PHILA., PA.

*A*LTHOUGH HE LACKS the name recognition of rookie standout Joe Jackson, Mike Mitchell rivals Shoeless Joe for the number-one spot on the Most Wanted list of E90-1 collectors.

importance, chest thrust forward, chin held high, a confident smile emerging. The Cincinnati Reds outfielder could easily pass for a player of Hall of Fame stature—and he was playing like one at the time. Mitchell averaged 19 triples,

leader. Mitchell retired in 1914 after eight steady seasons. He lived into his eighties and died on July 16, 1961, at which point his bright-yellow portrait was still *undocumented* in card listings. Today, of course, there are no "E" series

1909–1911 E90-1 American Caramel — Mike Mitchell

Mitchell is an inexplicably short-printed member of the seminal issue. He is American Caramel's white elephant, the lofty last hurdle on the road to set completion—the "Honus Wagner of 'E' Cards." Mitchell appears to sense his

86 RBI, and 36 stolen bases from 1909 to 1911, twice pacing the National League in three-baggers. Appropriately perhaps, his .310 batting average in 1909 was second only to Wagner, the senior circuit's perennial

aficionados unfamiliar with the prized rarity or unwilling to pay top dollar for one, regardless of condition.
Estimated Value: $5,000

Base Ball Gum.

THIS CARD IS ONE
OF A SET OF

50 Base Ball Players

PROMINENT MEM-
BERS OF NATIONAL
AND AMERICAN
LEAGUES, ONE OF
WHICH IS WRAP-
PED WITH EVERY
PACKAGE OF BASE
BALL GUM.

Manufactured only by
JOHN H. DOCKMAN & SONS

Matthewson, p. N. Y. Nat'l

CHRISTY MATHEWSON graces some of the hobby's most beautifully designed cards. In this horizontal masterpiece, familiar quality, perhaps evoking the closing sequence in *Field of Dreams*, when Ray and Roy Kinsella share an emotional father-son catch in the release of 40 cards (though the backs report 50). Mathewson, whose captioned name is misspelled with two t's, was at the apex of his career in 1909,

1909 E92 Dockman & Sons — Christy Mathewson

the setting sun casts its glow on the sky and land as Mathewson calmly releases a ball to his unseen throwing partner. The meditative scene has a timeless, gloaming before the camera pans away to a bird's-eye view. Candy-card collectors will immediately recognize this depiction from the Dockman & Sons having won his second Triple Crown the previous season with an astounding 37 wins, 259 strikeouts, and 1.43 ERA. *Estimated Value: $2,500*

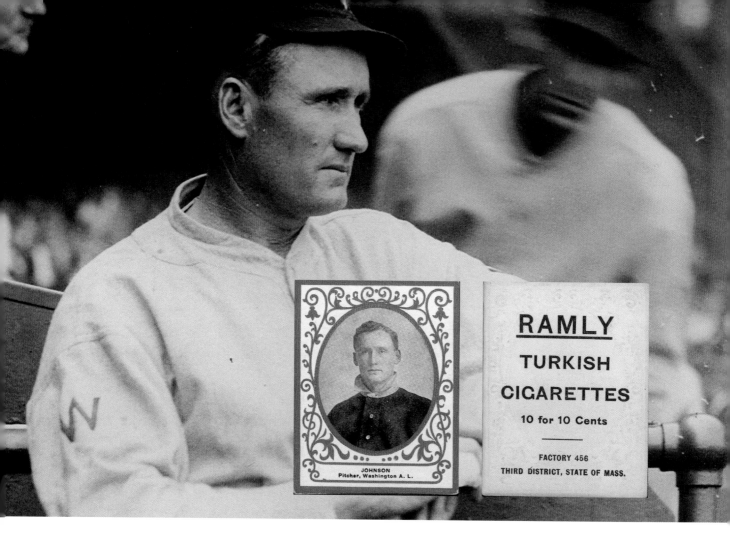

*H*ISTORICALLY, RAMLYS were best avoided. Their scarcity was prohibitive, their design esoteric, and their roster disappointing. That a 1909 tobacco issue could leave out marquee names such as Ty Cobb, Honus Wagner, Christy Mathewson, and Nap Lajoie was viewed as a dire tragedy. In their stead, the 121-card set featured its era's second-tier stars—Three Finger Brown, Chief Bender, Johnny Evers, and their ilk—along with little-known players like Barney Pelty, Bill Shipke, Admiral Schlei, and Walter Johnson. In three years with the Washington Senators, Johnson had authored 32 wins against 48 losses. His worst campaign, a 13-25 showing, came the same year that Ramly Turkish Cigarettes chose to include him in their unusual production. It was beyond the ken of manufacturers or collectors that the Kansas native was destined for greatness. His unassuming portrait, by master photographer Carl Horner, betrays nothing of the intensity and fortitude that would spawn Johnson's nickname "The Big Train"; nothing of the ensuing 10 straight seasons of 20-plus wins, highlighted by a 36-7 mark in 1913; nothing of his second-best 417 career victories and his unattainable 110 shutouts. Needless to say, Johnson has since become the centerpiece of the T204s, an issue which has all but lost its early stigma. Today, hobbyists adjudge the gold-filigreed Ramlys to be a choice creation of the period. Although its gallery of subjects still leaves a noticeable void, the Ramly set is championed for its majestic, delicate design and its consequent status as a daunting high-grade quest among set-builders.
Estimated Value: $7,500

1909 T204 Ramly — Walter Johnson

BASE BALL STARS
This card is one of a set of 30 stars from original photographs
1. AMES, New York National
2. BENDER, Phila. American
3. BROWN, Chicago National
4. COLLINS, Phila. American
5. CHANCE, Chicago National
6. COVELESKIE, Cincinnati Nat'l
7. CHASE, New York American
8. COBB, Detroit American
9. CLARKE, Pittsburg National
10. DELEHANTY, Detroit American
11. DONOVAN, Detroit American
12. DOOIN, Philadelphia National
13. EVERS, Chicago National
14. GIBSON, Pittsburg National
15. GRIFFITH, Cincinnati National
16. JENNINGS, Detroit American
17. JONES, Detroit American
18. JOSS, Cleveland American
19. LAJOIE, Cleveland American
20. LEACH, Pittsburg National
21. MATHEWSON, N. Y. National
22. McGRAW, New York National
23. PHILLIPPI, Pittsburg National
24. PLANK, Philadelphia American
25. PASTORIOUS, Brooklyn Nat'l
26. TINKER, Chicago National
27. WADDELL, St. Louis American
28. WAGNER, Pittsburg National
29. WILTSE, New York National
30. CY. YOUNG, Cleveland Amer.
Manufactured only by
Standard Caramel Co., Lancaster, Pa.

TINKER. CHICAGO NAT'L

A NOTHER STRONG entry in the series of confectionery issues preceding World War I was Standard Caramel's 1910 offering, classified as E93. Candy cards are generally smaller than their tobacco contemporaries in four ways: physical dimensions, production runs, roster sizes, and available populations—all of which result in scarce, condition-sensitive sets that are dense with Hall of Famers and rife with bright, candy-like colors. Standard Caramel hewed closely to the formula. Cubs shortstop Joe Tinker's card-front sports a fiery mélange of orange and red, while the checklist on the back identifies among the edition's 30 subjects such big-name figures as Ty Cobb, Napoleon Lajoie, Christy Mathewson, Honus Wagner, and Cy Young—not to mention Tinker's double-play accomplices Johnny Evers and Frank Chance. The 1910 season was a typically solid campaign for Tinker, who converted 94 percent of his fielding plays and also, on June 28, swiped home plate twice in one game. In 1914, he jumped ship to the short-lived Federal League as player/manager of the Chicago Whales, before closing out his career with one season at the Cubs' helm.
Estimated Value: $500

1910 E93 STANDARD CARAMEL — JOE TINKER

"THE MILLION-DOLLAR Card." This is the one that garners front-page news worldwide, the one on which the hobby is founded and bases its reputation of legitimacy. Without Wagner, baseball

writer reciprocated Wagner's mannerly gesture by never cashing the check.) That article notwithstanding, conspiracy theorists hold firm to the idea that tobacco ethics was not the culprit here; rather, Wagner, arguably the game's

1996, CNN broadcasted a live drawing of finalist entries and announced Florida postal worker Patricia Gibbs as the winning contestant. Unable to pay the taxes on her prize, Gibbs auctioned the card through Sotheby's for

1909–1911 T206 White Border — Honus Wagner

cards might have remained in the company of other childhood pastimes that became collectors' items, like toys, model trains, and lunch pails, instead of joining the elite ranks of coins, documents, and fine art. This diminutive tobacco insert is the cardboard equivalent of the 1804 silver dollar, Christopher Columbus' signature, and Vincent Van Gogh's artwork.

There are fewer than 100 known examples of the T206 White Border Honus Wagner. Industry experts agree that the American Tobacco Trust halted the printing of Wagner's card early in the set's three-year production period. Theories abound as to why the card was struck from the issue, but the prevailing notion—that Wagner found the endorsing of cigarettes to be morally objectionable (even though he himself enjoyed chewing tobacco)—originates from an article published in an October 24, 1912, issue of *The Sporting News*. So the story goes, American Tobacco had hired a Pittsburgh sportswriter to broker Wagner's endorsement deal. The Pirates shortstop promptly refused the financial arrangement, but not without sending the representative a $10 check to compensate the man for the amount he had been promised by his employer. (Reportedly, the sports-

biggest star at the time, was unhappy with the royalties (or lack thereof) for the use of his image and thus nixed the deal. Either way, the mystery only adds to the card's mystique.

Any surviving example, no matter how weathered by time, is worth upwards of $50,000, even if only as a status symbol. But there is a single specimen, pictured here, that outdistances all others: "The Gretzky Wagner." This gem first made headlines back in 1991, when Wayne Gretzky and L.A. Kings owner Bruce McNall bought the card in a Sotheby's auction for the then-astronomical sum of $451,000, setting off a media blitzkrieg. Anyone unfamiliar with cardboard collectibles was shocked if not appalled, but insiders understood completely. Not only was the specimen in pristine condition, but it was also one of a select few Wagners to feature advertising on the reverse for Piedmont Cigarettes, instead of the customary ad for Sweet Caporal Cigarettes. That one-two combination added up to the best T206 Honus Wagner on the planet. Several years later, the Gretzky/McNall partnership privately sold their investment so that it could be used as a sales promotion by Wal-Mart. On Wagner's birthday (February 24) in

$640,500. And four years later, the Gretzky Wagner's new owner ushered in the second millennium with a consignment to Robert Edward Auctions, then a division of MastroNet Premier Auctions. The card finally broke through its hobby's glass ceiling of a million dollars, peaking at $1,265,000 once furious bidding gave way to the gavel.

Now, it would be easy to cast off these kingly sums as showy one-upmanship, frivolous extravagance, or our modern-day infatuation with gross excess, but the Wagner has *always* been the preeminent treasure in the pantheon of card classics. It is the backbone of the industry, holding court in the spheres of rarity, value, and Mona Lisa-like iconography. Someday, the T206 White Border Honus Wagner may well be deemed the *Ten*-Million Dollar Card!

Estimated Value: $500,000

*L*IKE HONUS WAGNER, Eddie Plank is sorely underrepresented among existing T206 cards—and no one knows why. Did the Philadelphia A's hurler object to endorsing tobacco, as many have postulated about Wagner? Did Plank hold out for higher royalty payments? Were his cards perhaps hoarded by rival Red Sox fans and ceremoniously tossed into the harbor during the Boston

strong, contains a cornucopia of different cardback designs promoting cigarette companies with such colorful names as Hindu, Broad Leaf, Lenox, Drum, Carolina Brights, Lenox, Piedmont, and Uzit. The brands were competitors—but only by name. For in actuality, they were all commercially linked to the "American Tobacco Trust" conglomerate. Although a scant few Plank cards have Piedmont backs (lead-

ken plate" notion: Most of Plank's Sweet Caporal backs are of the "150 Series" variety, meaning that his was one of only 150 designs that had been printed so far. Other copies, however, say "350 Subjects." Evidently, the plate survived long enough for the card to continue well past the earliest stages of production. And so the mystery remains as to why popular Eddie Plank, the most successful southpaw of his generation, the

1909-1911 T206 White Border — Eddie Plank

PLANK, PHILA. AMER.

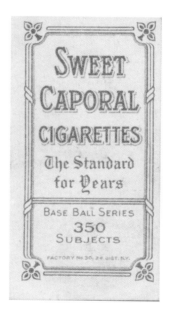

"Tea206" Party?! The most readily accepted explanation faults a broken printing plate at the factory. But even the "broken plate" theory is spurious at best, in large part because of the advertisements on the reverse of Plank's 100 or so known specimens. The T206 White Border set, more than 525 cards

ing conspiracy theorists to surmise that he and Honus were printed on the same Piedmont factory sheets, and that Plank may have been an unwitting casualty of Wagner's production halt), the overwhelming majority carries an ad for Sweet Caporal Cigarettes. Herein lies the shattering of the "bro-

winner of 326 mound appearances and six pennants, would be such a missing face in a card issue that should be rife with his high-collared, youthful portrait. Has anyone checked the bottom of Boston Harbor?
Estimated Value: $30,000

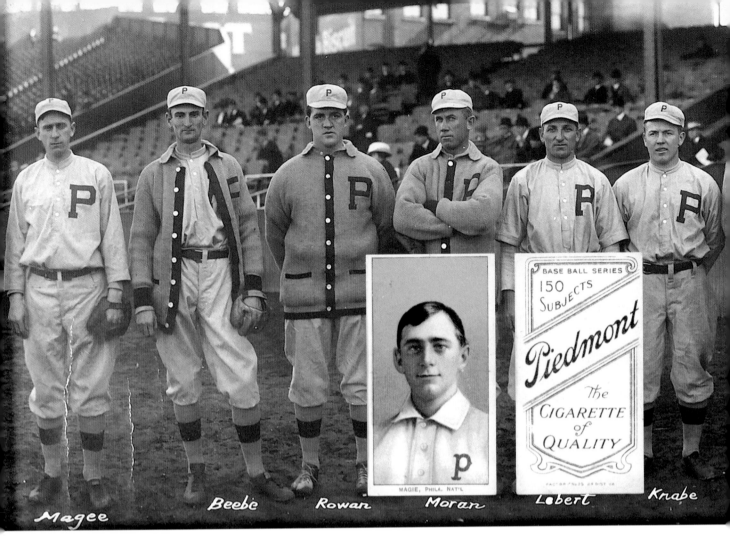

Magee   Beebe   Rowan   Moran   Lobert   Knabe

S HAKESPEARE WROTE, "What's in a name? That which we call a rose by any other word would smell as sweet." Not so in the realm of baseball cards, where a name—or even a letter within that name—may make all the difference in the world. Just ask Sherry Magee. The hobby's most illustrious "error" card, Magee complements Honus Wagner, Eddie Plank, and Joe Doyle as the "Big Four" of the T206 White Borders. Each member of the quartet is prohibitively rarer than the rest of the set. Although there are numerous theories, the jury is still out on why Wagner and Plank exist in such scant numbers. As for Magee, the reason is clear and boils down to a single vowel—the typesetter bought an "I" instead of an "E." Brief distribution ensued before the misspelling was discovered and corrected. All of the "Magie" variations have a Piedmont Cigarettes advertisement on the back and, like their three "Big" brothers, are high-demand commodities regardless of condition. Outfielder Sherry Magee played 16 solid seasons (1904-1919), once leading the National League in batting and four times in RBI. His final at-bat came with the Cincinnati Reds in the infamous 1919 World Series, which the Reds won over the Chicago "Black Sox" five games to three.
Estimated Value: $15,000

1909-1911 T206 White Border Variation — Sherry Magee

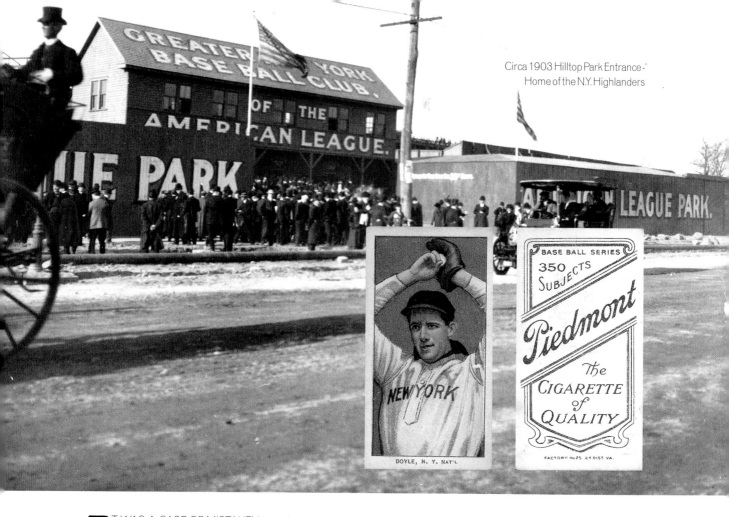

Circa 1903 Hilltop Park Entrance ·
Home of the N.Y. Highlanders

DOYLE, N. Y. NAT'L

BASE BALL SERIES
350 SUBJECTS
Piedmont
The CIGARETTE of QUALITY

FACTORY No.25 2ª DIST. VA.

*I*T WAS A CASE OF MISTAKEN identity that vaulted "Slow Joe" Doyle from obscurity to renown as one-quarter of the T206 set's elite Big Four. Doyle's first cards to roll off the printing press identified his team notoriety outside the Big Apple—except that the "Hands Over Head" pose should have been a clear sign this was not Larry, a second baseman, but rather Joe, a pitcher. No one knows how many of these error cards were manu-

intrepid enough to pursue the assembly of a "master set" containing all known standard-issue and variation cards in the monumental White Border series. Six years ago, one Doyle in particular sold at auction for more than

1909–1911 T206 White Border "Hands Over Head" Variation — Joe Doyle

and league as "N.Y. NAT'L." The fact was, Joe Doyle suited up for the New York Highlanders of the American League; *Larry* Doyle belonged to the National League's New York Giants. The gaffe was a reasonable one—both players had broken into baseball within recent years and had achieved little

factured before the "NAT'L" was removed from the caption, but those that have been discovered heretofore number fewer than a half dozen—making Doyle's abridged production rarer than Honus Wagner, Eddie Plank, or Sherry Magee. Its near absence has raised the stakes for any hobbyist

$175,000, quadrupling its estimated value at that time. And so, while his doppelganger Larry Doyle enjoyed a superior, 14-year career in the majors, Joe Doyle, lifetime winner of 22 games in five seasons, is the Doyle who will be remembered for the ages.
Estimated Value: $75,000

WHILE HONUS Wagner was boycotting the use of his image as an endorsement for tobacco (or so the story goes), Ty Cobb was busy reveling in the use of his own. To start, Cobb be "King of the Smoking Tobacco World"—as if to say with a sneer, *Put that in your pipe and smoke it, Honus!* About a dozen examples are thought to exist with the Ty Cobb backs, making them more elusive even than the fabled T206 front surface from tobacco residue. The near-pristine exemplar pictured here bears no such veneer, signifying that it was actually an unreleased "proof" card. In 1909, the first year of issue for T206, Cobb was more than just a sover-

1909-1911 T206 White Border with Ty Cobb Reverse — Ty Cobb

COBB, DETROIT

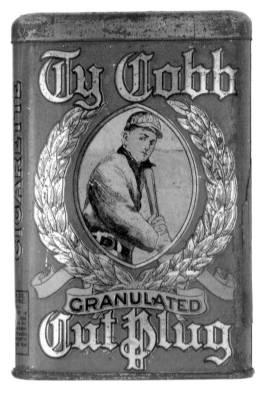

"TY COBB" KING OF THE SMOKING TOBACCO WORLD.

FACTORY N° 33-4, DIST. OF N.C.

occupies no less than four different card designs in the T206 White Border set—a red-background portrait, a green-background portrait, a bat-on-shoulder pose, and a bat-off-shoulder pose. Furthermore, the red-background style comes in a virtually never-seen back variation declaring Cobb to Wagner and ranking them as one of the hobby's highest-prized depictions of the Georgia Peach. Each one of the rarities was originally distributed in a Ty Cobb-brand tobacco tin—now considered the Holy Grail for collectors of vintage baseball tins—and was given a special glossy coating to protect the card's eign of the "Smoking Tobacco World." He was also king of the American League, his .377 average, 9 home runs and 107 RBI worthy of the exalted Triple Crown.
Estimated Value: $30,000

1910 E125 American Caramel Die-Cuts — Honus Wagner

PITTSBURGH'S FLYING Dutchman delivers both a batting stance and a fielding pose in this exceedingly rare, damage-prone release of large die-cut candy cards. There are 42 entries in all, each printed on heavy cardboard with the purpose of freestanding display. Text on the reverse provides a checklist for the respective player's team and a sales pitch by manufacturer American Caramel that one card "is given free with each of our Action Picture Caramels."

Among the depicted subjects from the Pirates, Red Sox, Giants, and Athletics, Wagner and his fellow Buccaneers surely would have been in greatest demand among consumers. The reigning major-league champions had overcome Ty Cobb's Detroit Tigers in a seven-game battle at the 1909 World Series. Wagner had meted out 8 hits in 24 at-bats for a .333 average, slightly below his regular-season batting clip of .339 and a tad above his lifetime mark of .329. The 1909 title would be the first and only championship of his phenomenal 21-season career.

Estimated Value: $5,000

1911 E94 Close Candy — Cy Young

"OLD" CY YOUNG, INDEED. The patriarch of mound dominance and durability turned 44 in 1911, his last of 22 seasons in the majors. Young split the curtain-call campaign between his two adopted cities, Cleveland and Boston, pitching for the Naps and Rustlers, respectively, as opposed to his former Cleveland Spiders and Boston Pilgrims. Though twice as old as many of the batsmen he encountered, Young still mustered a decent 7-9 record in 18 starts, with 2 shutouts and 55 strike-outs. This action pose of the "Canton Cyclone" rifling his millionth or so professional pitch is set against several different background-color varieties, each equally striking, within the 30-subject E94 set. The issue's attribution to the George Close Company of Cambridge, Massachusetts, does not emanate from any standard copyright line on the reverse-side checklist. Rather, a proportion of the series displays an ink-stamped "overprint" on the reverse, with baseball-related slogans such as "YOUR (sic) OUT! if you don't eat Close's Oppie Dildocks," or "CLOSE'S CANDIES are Pennant Winners." These overprinted copies often elicit a higher premium than their unstamped brethren.

Estimated Value: $2,000

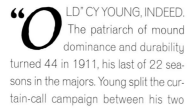

"OLD" CY. YOUNG, CLEVELAND

This card is one of a set of Star Base Ball Players' Cards as follows :

MOORE, Philadelphia National
GRANT, Cincinnati National
MURRAY, New York National
BYRNE, Pittsburg National
CRAWFORD, Detroit American
AUSTIN, New York American
"JOE" LAKE, St. Louis National
LOBERT, Philadelphia National
MAGEE, New York National
"HUGH" JENNINGS, Det. American
DOOLAN, Philadelphia National
"OLD" CY YOUNG, Cleveland Amer.
"HARRY" DAVIS, Phila. American
McGRAW, New York National
"TY" COBB, Detroit American
"TOMMY" LEACH, Pittsburg Natl.
LORD, Chicago American
DOUGHERTY, New York American
LAJOIE, Cleveland American
DEVORE, New York National
CHANCE, Chicago American
CICOTTE, Boston American
BATES, Philadelphia National
"HANS" WAGNER, Pittsburg Nat.
SPEAKER, Boston American
KLEINOW, New York American
BESCHER, Cincinnati National
TURNER, Cleveland American
EVERS, Chicago National
DEVLIN, New York National

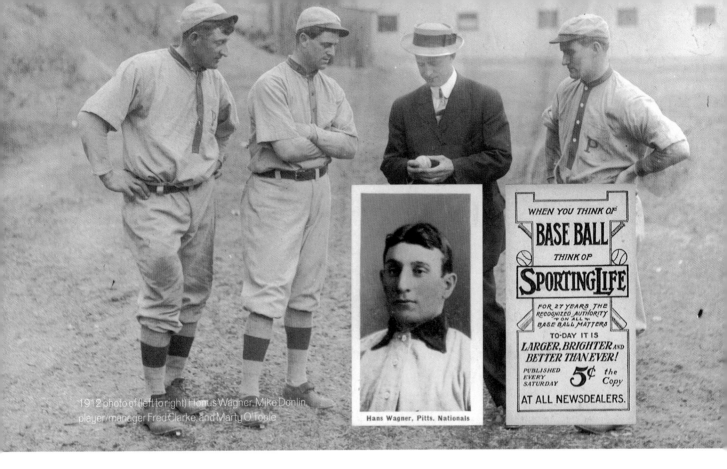

1912 photo of (left to right) Honus Wagner, Mike Donlin, player/manager Fred Clarke, and Marty O'Toole

Hans Wagner, Pitts. Nationals

WHEN YOU THINK OF
BASE BALL
THINK OF
SPORTINGLIFE
FOR 27 YEARS THE RECOGNIZED AUTHORITY ON ALL BASE BALL MATTERS
TO-DAY IT IS
LARGER, BRIGHTER AND BETTER THAN EVER!
PUBLISHED EVERY SATURDAY 5¢ the Copy
AT ALL NEWSDEALERS.

THIS CARD BEGS A double-take. *Isn't that the...hold on a minute...since when did the T206 Wagner, that crown jewel of the hobby, change its color scheme?* Fact is, the so-called "Million Dollar Card" and its contemporary counterpart, seen here, are similar in size and share an identical portrait by photographer Carl Horner. In terms of their origin and distribution, however, they could hardly differ more. The T206 was an "insert" produced by the American Tobacco Trust and found inside (not many, as it were) packs of cigarettes. The M116 was issued by *Sporting Life* magazine as a "premium" available to its readers.

A colossal undertaking, even for such a well-established, 27-year-old publication, the 288-subject assembly included 24 series of 12 cards apiece. As one might expect, the earlier series were packed with marquee names and redeemed in greater numbers than the later, now-scarcer segments. Harry Hooper and Tris Speaker are the sole "high number" Hall of Famers, their appearances forestalled until the penultimate, twenty-third series. Although Wagner was one of the very first entries, this particular copy was actually introduced *after* those of Hooper and Speaker, when *Sporting Life* reprinted the 24 cards of the first two series with a blue background instead of the standard "pastel" design. Another interesting variation occurred on the dozen entries in the third series, where the magazine's advertisement on the reverses is occasionally printed in blue

1910-1911 M116 Sporting Life Blue Background — Honus Wagner

ink, rather than black. Add to those 36 anomalies a pair of subjects, Amby McConnell and George McQuillan (who were traded mid-production and whose cards were updated to reflect the transactions) and the original scope of 288 cards crests at a "master set" grand total of 326.

Estimated Value: $2,000

1910 New Orleans Pelicans with Joe Jackson (seated, third from right)

SERIES No. 8

OLD MILL CIGARETTES

BASE BALL SUBJECTS

LARGE ASSORTMENT

FACTORY N° 25, 2 ª DIST. VA.

MOST MINOR-league depictions of major-league stars are dubbed "pre-rookie" cards. Not Joe Jackson's portrait with the New Orleans Pelicans, however, for cess to come with the Naps and Chicago White Sox. After outgrowing New Orleans, Jackson wouldn't play for another team below the big-league level until after his banishment from baseball, when he occasionally suited the Mason-Dixon line and each less talent-rich than the next. Why modern collectors flock to this production stems from its difficulty and condition sensitivity. It is an heir-apparent to the large and elusive Old Judge series of the 1880s,

1910 T210 OLD MILL — JOE JACKSON

Shoeless Joe had already logged 10 games over two seasons with Connie Mack's Philadelphia Athletics, and had previously made his professional card debut in American Caramel's 1909 E90-1 release. Does that make this his "*post*-pre-rookie"? Preposterous! Jackson led the Pelicans to a Southern Association title in 1910, then rejoined the majors for the Cleveland Naps' final 20 games of the season. He hit .387 with 5 triples—a sure sign of the suc-

up for sold-out barnstorming games in small towns. His three-quarter-length image in Old Mill's tobacco issue catches the still-unproven batsman wearing his early allegiance on his sleeve, an "N-O" insignia matching that of his pillbox-style cap. Beyond Jackson and 20-year-old outfielder Casey Stengel, the immense, red-bordered set of 640 subjects is defined by mediocrity. Represented therein are eight different minor leagues, each situated below

as well as a logical next step for conquistadors of the 1909-11 White Border and Gold Border tobacco editions. Jackson alone restricts many an Old Mill enthusiast from reaching set completion. Only a scant number of copies are thought to have survived, elevating this treasure to the ranks of Honus Wagner and Eddie Plank as one of the premier tobacco cards of the hobby. *Estimated Value: $100,000*

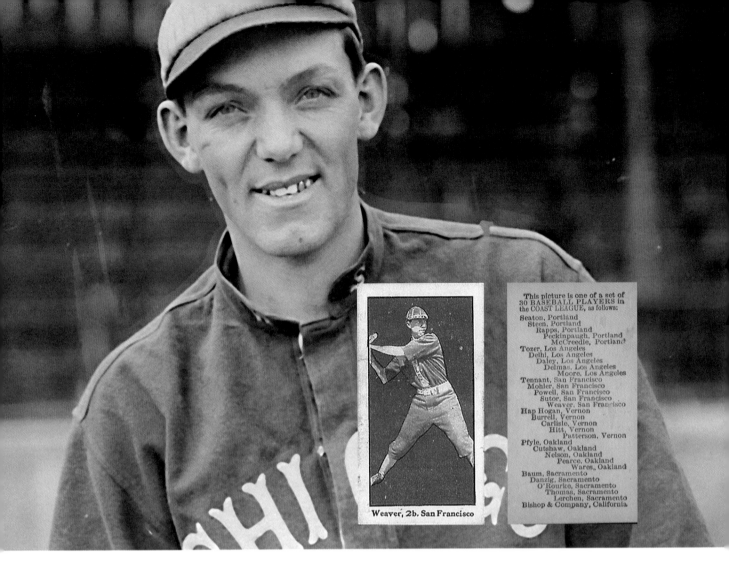

This picture is one of a set of
30 BASEBALL PLAYERS in
the COAST LEAGUE, as follows:

Seaton, Portland
Steen, Portland
Rapps, Portland
Peckinpaugh, Portland
McCreedie, Portland
Tozer, Los Angeles
Delhi, Los Angeles
Daley, Los Angeles
Delmas, Los Angeles
Moore, Los Angeles
Tennant, San Francisco
Mohler, San Francisco
Powell, San Francisco
Sutor, San Francisco
Weaver, San Francisco
Hap Hogan, Vernon
Burrell, Vernon
Carlisle, Vernon
Hitt, Vernon
Patterson, Vernon
Pfyle, Oakland
Cutshaw, Oakland
Nelson, Oakland
Pearce, Oakland
Wares, Oakland
Baum, Sacramento
Danzig, Sacramento
O'Rourke, Sacramento
Thomas, Sacramento
Lerchen, Sacramento
Bishop & Company, California

Weaver, 2b. San Francisco

BUCK WEAVER WAS THE most notable—or, rather, notorious—alumnus of Bishop's 30-card set. Five ballplayers from each team in the Pacific Coast League (PCL) made the cut, with Weaver a delegate of the San Francisco Seals. Collectors adore the regional release for its action images, dramatic background colors, and stark exclusivity. Weaver matriculated from the PCL to the Majors in 1912, won a starting spot at shortstop for the Chicago White Sox, and held the position for his next nine seasons with the Pale Hose. Like his teammate Joe Jackson, Weaver gave a strong showing in the 1919 World Series. He batted .324 with four doubles and committed no fielding errors, a performance suggesting Weaver wasn't in on the "fix." Then, boosted either by a clear conscience or by raging guilt, he had his best year yet in 1920, setting career highs in batting average (.324), hits (208), and doubles (34). Alas, Weaver never took the field again. He went down swinging as one of the "Eight Men Out," and not because he had accepted any money for the World Series chicanery, but rather because he had been aware of the scheme and chose to guard the secret.

Estimated Value: $2,000

1911 E100 BISHOP AND COMPANY PCL — BUCK WEAVER

TURKEY REDS ARE HAILED BY many as the most attractive production of the early-twentieth century, if not of all time. The masterful lithography of the 1910s period is best experienced in such a large, cabinet-style format (5-3/4" x 8"), and the artistic have long understood that the prospect of redemption entices buyers, most of whom will never actually bring their quest to fruition. Everyday inserts can be passively, even accidentally acquired; elite premiums are actively pursued. In 1911, the two most coveted entries in

1911 T3 Turkey Red Cabinets
No. 9 – Ty Cobb

portrayals are unsurpassed in their elegance or aesthetic allure. At the core of the issue's time-transcending success lie its inherent advantages as a "premium." Redeemed with coupons from Turkey Red, Fez, and Old Mill cigarettes, the 100-card set were Christy Mathewson and Ty Cobb. It is a testament to the Turkey Red set's artistic genius that the menacing, antagonistic, embittered Cobb could somehow seem so docile. Gazing at the Tiger batsman, posed in an

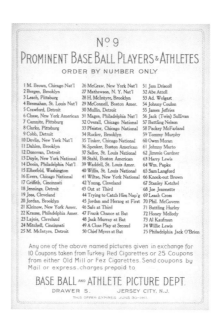

the cabinets were never inserted directly within packages of tobacco products. Therefore, they did not have to conform to any unwavering standards on dimensions, materials, or print runs. The cards could be created in a large size and with a higher level of quality. Akin to the phenomenon of factory rebates, manufacturers empty ballpark against a glowing, rose-inflected sunset, his cleats firmly planted instead of slashing toward a baseman, his expression serene instead of snarling, one actually understands how he might have earned such a genteel nickname as "The Georgia Peach."
Estimated Value: $20,000

BECAUSE OF THEIR COMparable design, dimensions, and artistic beauty, *Sporting Life* cabinets and Turkey Red cabinets are often closely linked by collectors. One difference between the two pro-

Life siblings number just six ballplayers—Ty Cobb, Christy Mathewson, Napoleon Lajoie, Honus Wagner, Hal Chase, and Frank Chance—and, on the whole, have a far scarcer population. In Chance's lush rendering, the Chicago

its readers with "Action Pictures" in exchange for mail-in coupons, Chance enjoyed his penultimate, seventh season as player/manager of the Cubs. The "Peerless Leader" had marshaled his team to a record 116 wins in 1906,

1911 M110 Sporting Life Cabinets — Frank Chance

ductions rests in classification, *Sporting Life* being a weekly newspaper and Turkey Red a cigarette company. The second essential distinction is quantity, both in terms of card subjects and available copies. Turkey Reds picture 100 different players and are relatively obtainable in the hobby; their *Sporting*

Cubs first baseman leisurely completes a throw to a teammate. It's an interesting choice of pose considering that Chance was better known for his glove than his arm, occupying the final destination of the storied double-play combination Tinker to Evers to Chance. In 1911, the year *Sporting Life* awarded

four National League pennants (1906-1908, 1910), and two championships (1907-1908), all the while distinguishing himself as one of the game's most judicious and respected strategists. *Estimated Value: $2,000*

Miller Huggins (right) with Connie Mack.

THE RUBRIC BEHIND Double Folders was that two teammates occupied each card and, to do so, shared one pair of legs. A factory-made horizontal fold about neck high on Miller Huggins allowed

the card's front side, with or without the requisite folding, so too did the Mecca Cigarettes advertising/statistical panel remain visible at all times on the reverse. Collector fascination with this issue is high today not only because of its lovely

"The Duke of Tralee," garnered his Cooperstown induction on the merits of versatile play, defensive prowess, and leadership. Short-statured second baseman Hug, or "Mighty Mite," would earn his nod from the Veterans'

1911 T201 MECCA DOUBLE FOLDERS — MILLER HUGGINS/ROGER BRESNAHAN

the upper half of Roger Bresnahan's body to hinge over top of the card's front. This configuration would obscure Huggins in favor of Bresnahan until the new flap—which, incidentally, altered the card's length but not its width—was lifted back to the original position. And just as the legs are constantly in view on

pastel artwork, but also due to the relative attainability of assembling a complete set. There are 50 total cards showcasing 100 different figures—among them some minor leaguers. In 1911, future Hall of Famers Huggins and Bresnahan were teammates on the St. Louis Cardinals. Bresnahan, dubbed

Committee for his managerial tenure, first as the Cardinals' player-manager and then as the Yankees' skipper throughout the Ruth-Gehrig dynasty decade of the 1920s.
Estimated Value: $200

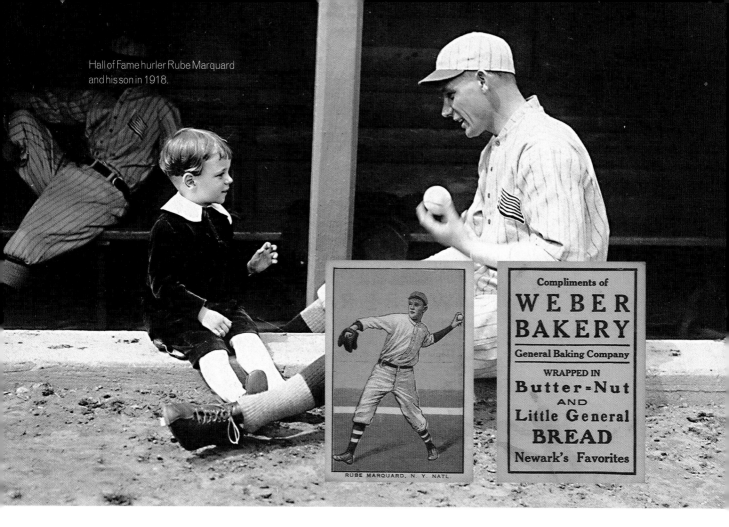

Hall of Fame hurler Rube Marquard and his son in 1918.

Compliments of
WEBER BAKERY
General Baking Company
WRAPPED IN
Butter=Nut
AND
Little General
BREAD
Newark's Favorites

RUBE MARQUARD, N. Y. NATL.

ESTLED IN AMONG the multiple tobacco-card editions of the early 1910s is a modest set of 25 subjects that were regionally distributed inside loaves of packaged bread. And just as the behemoth American Tobacco Trust marketed its collectibles under subsidiaries like Piedmont and Turkey Red, so too was there an overarching entity behind the brand-names Brunners, Butter Krust, and Weber Bakery: the General Baking Company. Jefferson

Burdick's *American Card Catalog* christened the series D304 and, historically, the consensus has been that General Baking's offering originated in 1911. Truth be told, though, its date of birth was more likely 1912 because (a) several of the set's players were traded late in the 1911 season and their card captions reflect the new team affiliations, and (b) the set's roster is heavily weighted with representatives of the 1911 pennant-winning Philadelphia Athletics and New York Giants. Giants

southpaw Rube Marquard clearly made the cut on the strength of his 1911 numbers. The high-profile young recruit had previously endured three disappointing seasons when he suddenly turned his career around with win totals of 24, 26, and 23 from 1911 to 1913. Eighteen big-league campaigns, 201 mound victories, and some key friends on the Hall of Fame Veterans Committee ultimately catapulted Marquard to Cooperstown in 1971. *Estimated Value: $1,500*

1911–1914 D304 WEBER BAKERY — RUBE MARQUARD

THIS GENTEEL PORTRAIT of Joe McGinnity belies the New York Giants pitcher's rugged reputation. Behind the neatly combed hair and Ivy League veneer was a steely competitor whose "Iron

8 mark and 1.61 earned run average. McGinnity's one decade of big-league play garnered a 1946 Hall of Fame induction, yet covers less than half of his unorthodox baseball career. Rather than retire, the "Iron Man" went back to

1912 C46 Imperial Tobacco – Joe McGinnity

Man" nickname derived from his indefatigable work ethic on the mound and his off-season labor at a foundry. McGinnity compressed 246 wins into a mere 10 seasons. In August of 1903, he drew attention for pitching both full games of doubleheaders not once, not twice, but three times in a single month. The next year he posted a stunning 35-

the minors. He pitched for small-town teams throughout the 1910s (often with ballclubs he also either managed or part-owned) and even moonlighted for the Dubuque squad of the Mississippi Valley League as late as 1925, at age 54. Canadian manufacturer Imperial Tobacco Company featured McGinnity early on in that second

phase of his playing days, while with the Eastern League's Newark club. The classy, wood-bordered, 90-subject release stands as the only baseball tobacco-card set that was ever issued in Canada.
Estimated Value: $500

IF TY COBB WAS THE RESIdent troublemaker of early-twentieth-century baseball, then Christy Mathewson was, in literary parlance, Cobb's foil character. Matty held sway as the game's Golden Boy.

national pastime—and our nation. When the advertising world knocked at his door, Mathewson became the ideal spokesman for numerous companies, many of which utilized the moundsman's iconic image from the 1911

1911 T205 Gold Border – Christy Mathewson

Beyond even his 373 wins, two pitching Triple Crowns (1905, 1908), 2.13 career ERA, and three complete-game shutouts in a single World Series (1905), Matty was dashingly handsome, invariably courteous, and wildly popular. He was lionized by younger and older fans alike as an embodiment of everything that was decent about our

T205 Gold Border set. A Mona Lisa-like half smile and a knowing gaze give the portrait an air of intrigue, while the boyish features, loosely fitting cap, and cascading curl of hair cement Matty's reputation as the clean-cut idol of his generation.
Estimated Value: $1,000

"Confluence of Greatness" - (left to right) Lou Gehrig, Tris Speaker, Ty Cobb, and Babe Ruth in 1928.

THERE ARE THREE DIStinct designs among the Gold Borders—one for the American League (seen here), a second for the National League (seen in Christy Mathewson's case), and a third for the minor leagues. With all due respect to Matty and his senior-circuit kin, the American Leaguers' style is superior. Each junior-circuit entry constitutes a work of art, marrying luxurious colors with an intricately balanced layout. Like Mathewson's card, the size is diminutive, the perimeter gilded, and the top two corners festooned with the team's insignia and moniker. That is where the similarities end. A scroll, rather than a facsimile signature, conveys Cobb's name, and it is enfolded by period equipment—a glove, two bats, a mask, and a stitched orb. Cobb's countenance centers a baseball-diamond interior that, on a larger scale, could pass for a Tiger fan's kite on a blustery World Series morning. The biographical sketch on the reverse pegs Cobb as "one of the fastest ball players that ever stepped on a diamond...lightning on the bases, only absolutely perfect throws ever stopping him." Of course, even as tobacco buyers read those words, the "Georgia Peach" was compounding his elite stature. In one of the game's finest individual performances, Cobb paced the league in 1911 with a .420 batting average, 248 hits, 47 doubles, 24 triples, 127 RBI, 147 runs, and 83 stolen bases. Those unprecedented statistics and the card's artful flair have conspired to make this beauty the pinnacle member of the Gold Border issue—which, devoid of any rarities on par with the "Big Four" of the T206 White Borders, is a much easier set to complete.

Estimated Value: $2,500

1911 T205 Gold Border — Ty Cobb

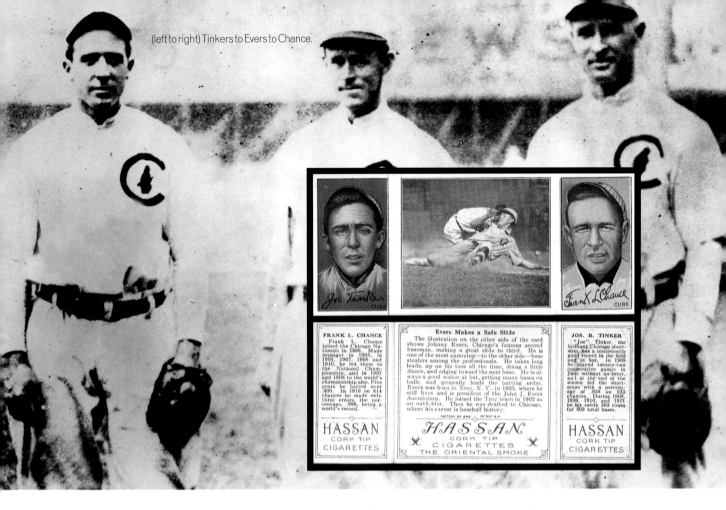

(left to right) Tinkers to Evers to Chance.

FRANK L. CHANCE
Frank L. Chance joined the Chicago Nationals in 1898. Made manager in 1905, in 1906, 1907, 1908 and 1910, he led them to the National Championship, and in 1907 and 1908 to the world's championship also. Five years he batted over .300. In 1910 on 814 chances he made only three errors, the percentage, .996, being a world's record.

Evers Makes a Safe Slide
The illustration on the other side of the card shows Johnny Evers, Chicago's famous second baseman, making a great slide to third. He is one of the most annoying—to the other side—base stealers among the professionals. He takes long leads, up on his toes all the time, doing a little dance, and edging toward the next base. He is always a good waiter at bat, getting many bases on balls, and generally leads the batting order. Evers was born in Troy, N. Y., in 1883, where he still lives and is president of the John J. Evers Association. He joined the Troy team in 1902 as an outfielder. Then he was drafted to Chicago, where his career is baseball history.

FACTORY N9 649   1ST DIST N.Y.

JOS. B. TINKER
"Joe" Tinker, the brilliant Chicago shortstop, has a consistently good record in the field and at bat. In 1908 he played twenty-two consecutive games in June without an error, and at the end of the season led the short-stops with a percent-age of .958 on 923 chances. During 1908, 1909, 1910, and 1911 he hit safely 563 times for 803 total bases.

HASSAN
CORK TIP
CIGARETTES

HASSAN
CORK TIP
CIGARETTES
THE ORIENTAL SMOKE

HASSAN
CORK TIP
CIGARETTES

T HREE NAMES LOOM largest in the annals of diamond double plays: Tinker, Evers, and Chance. And if ever there was a card production ideally suited to integral, central link. The radiant portraits originate from the previous year's T205 tobacco issue, while the black-and-white action shot, "Evers Makes a Safe Slide," was brought to life by mas-

These are the saddest of possible words:

"Tinker to Evers to Chance."

Trio of bear cubs, and fleeter than birds,

Tinker and Evers and Chance.

1912 T202 Hassan Triple Folders #64 "Evers Makes a Safe Slide" — Tinker/Evers/Chance

honor the Chicago Cubs triumvirate, it was the innovative set of triptychs sponsored by Hassan Cork-Tip Cigarettes. Shortstop Joe Tinker and first baseman Frank Chance are positioned as wingmen on the three-panel display, with second baseman Johnny Evers as their

ter lensman Charles M. Conlon. From left to right, the infielders are appropriately featured in the 6-4-3 combination immortalized by New York sportswriter Franklin Pierce Adams in his poem "Baseball's Sad Lexicon" (seen at right). *Estimated Value: $1,000*

Ruthlessly pricking our gonfalon bubble,

Making a Giant hit into a double --

Words that are heavy with nothing

but trouble:

"Tinker to Evers to Chance."

*T*HIS CENTRAL PANEL OF TY Cobb slashing into base is regarded as the greatest action shot in the history of our national pastime. A single black-and-white frame encapsulates Cobb's tenacity, prowess, and superior talent—and, likewise, that of the

thrown on his face. But in a moment I realized he wasn't hurt, and I was relieved...Then I began to wonder if by any chance I had snapped the play. I couldn't remember that I had, but I decided to play [it] safe and change plates anyway. I went home kicking myself. I said, 'Now, there was a great picture and you missed it.' I took out

1912 T202 Hassan Triple Folders #129 "Ty Cobb Steals Third" — Jennings/Cobb

legend behind the camera, Charles Conlon. In his own words, as quoted in Neal and Constance McCabe's book *Baseball's Golden Age: The Photographs of Charles M. Conlon,* Conlon recounts the turn of events thusly:

my plates and developed them. There was Cobb stealing third. In my excitement, I had snapped it, by instinct."

Tigers manager Hughie Jennings saw the fabled play, and may well have responded with his famous "Ee-yah" battle cry. Elected to the

"I was off third, chatting with Jimmy Austin, third baseman for the New York club. Cobb was on second, with one out, and the hitter was trying to bunt him to third. Austin moved in for the sacrifice. As Jimmy stood there, Cobb started. The fans shouted. Jimmy turned, backed into the base and was greeted by a storm of dirt, spikes, shoes, uniforms - and Ty Cobb. My first thought was that my friend, Austin, had been injured. When Cobb stole, he stole. Spikes flew and he did not worry where. I saw Ty's clenched teeth, his determined look. The catcher's peg went right by Jimmy, as he was

Hall of Fame as a player, Jennings was a lifetime .314 hitter who batted .401 in 1896 and captained his Baltimore Orioles to four consecutive bids for the Temple Cup championship (a nineteenth-century equivalent to the World Series). He took the helm for the Tigers in Cobb's third season, 1907, succinctly steered the club to three straight pennants, and retained his post until 1920, when he was replaced by, who else, Ty Cobb.

Estimated Value: $2,000

*L*OUIS LOWDERMILK? HERE is a name that might have been crunched underfoot by the endless parade of time, were it not for the somber series known as T207. Lowdermilk pitched two seasons for St.

Despite his lackluster career, "Lowdermilk" (as Louis is succinctly referred to among collectors) warrants reverential tones among hobbyists. He is the preeminent member of a T207 triumvirate dubbed the "Big Three,"

Lowdermilk's defense, however, the rendering does have its charms. His is a refreshingly bright portrayal in a set renowned for its dark-brown, funereal backdrop. The gangly, long-necked southpaw appears young and inno-

1912 T207 Brown Background — Louis Lowdermilk

Louis. He claimed four lifetime wins; he logged five career losses. Even the card's manufacturers had little of substance to say about him in their biography on the reverse:

which also features the similarly forgotten Irving Lewis and Ward Miller (both of whom, again, are identified with the least intimacy possible as "Lewis" and "Miller"). The trio's paramount importance, even with regard to such Hall of

cent, like the game itself. Louis Lowdermilk died in the mid-1970s at the age of 88, and one can only wonder how the lifetime 4-5 pitcher might have felt to learn that he was one of the most

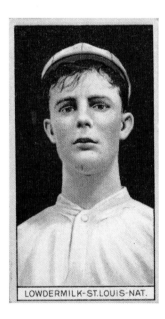

"Louis Lowdermilk, left handed pitcher for the St. Louis Nationals, stands six feet tall in baseball shoes and has a lot of speed which, as yet, is more or less untamed. His brother, Grover Lowdermilk, is even taller, and while both the Lowdermilk boys were with the Cardinals in 1911, Grover was dropped and Louis retained in 1912."

tance, even with regard to such Hall of Fame subjects as Tris Speaker and Walter Johnson, amounts to three key factors: rarity, rarity, rarity. Though the source of their dearth remains a question mark, it seems reasonable to assume that a causative link exists between the players' mediocrity and the paucity of their surviving cards. In

important figures in the annals of baseball cardboard.
Estimated Value: $5,000

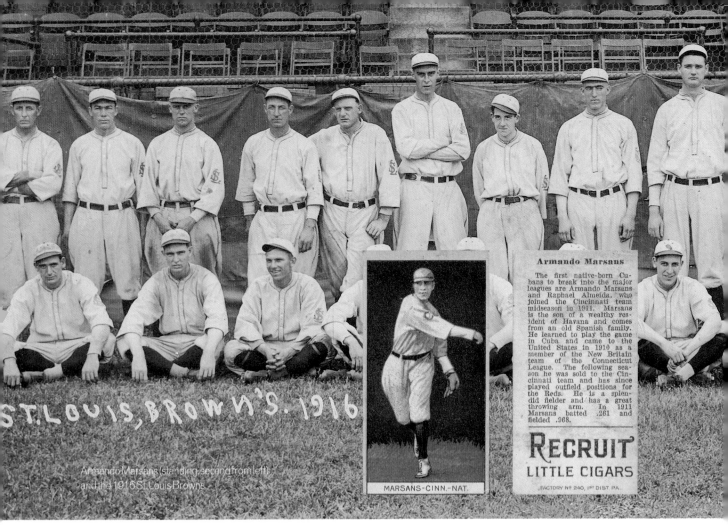

ST. LOUIS, BROWN'S. 1916

Armando Marsans (standing, second from left) and the 1916 St. Louis Browns.

Armando Marsans

The first native-born Cubans to break into the major leagues are Armando Marsans and Raphael Almeida, who joined the Cincinnati team midseason in 1911. Marsans is the son of a wealthy resident of Havana and comes from an old Spanish family. He learned to play the game in Cuba and came to the United States in 1910 as a member of the New Britain team of the Connecticut League. The following season he was sold to the Cincinnati team and has since played outfield positions for the Reds. He is a splendid fielder and has a great throwing arm. In 1911 Marsans batted .261 and fielded .968.

RECRUIT
LITTLE CIGARS
FACTORY Nº 240, 1ST DIST. PA.

MARSANS-CINN.-NAT.

BORN IN MATANZAS, Cuba, Armando Marsans played in the Negro Leagues and major leagues, his complexion and racial makeup—half-black—apparently ambiguous enough to qualify for both sides of the color line. Some have suggested that Marsans was Jackie Robinson's predecessor as the twentieth century's first black ballplayer in the majors, a far-fetched claim since Marsans' light skin did not expose him to the overt prejudice faced by Robinson, Larry Doby, and the game's other trailblazers of integration. Still, the signing of Marsans and fellow Cuban Rafael Almeida by Cincinnati Reds manager Clark Griffith (who insisted on the pair's Caucasian bloodline) does remain a formative step towards opening up the major leagues to all players regardless of race. Marsans quickly became a popular figure for his reliability in the field and his speed on the base paths. He appears on cardboard in both the 1912 T207 Brown Background and 1914–1915 Cracker Jack sets, with the former, seen here, dating to his best statistical season—a .317 average, 19 doubles, 7 triples, and 35 stolen bases. In 1914, Marsans challenged his Cincinnati contract by defecting to the upstart Federal League. He ultimately finished out his eight-year career with the St. Louis Browns and New York Yankees.
Estimated Value: $250

1912 T207 Brown Background —
Armando Marsans

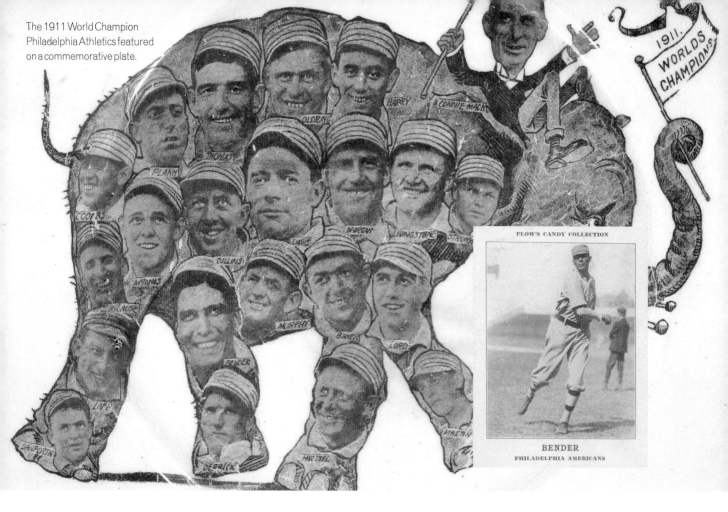

The 1911 World Champion Philadelphia Athletics featured on a commemorative plate.

PLOW'S CANDY COLLECTION

BENDER
PHILADELPHIA AMERICANS

AN ELUSIVE PRODUC-tion by the Plow's con-fection company receiv-ed the *American Card Catalog*'s final candy-card designation: E300. This, despite there being candy issues that discovered and checklisted in recent years. Plow's cards are noticeably larg-er than their tobacco-issue counter-parts, which gives the sepia images an especially commanding presence and resonance, on par perhaps with original American-Indians. He played the majority of his 16 seasons with Connie Mack's Philadelphia A's, notched 212 career victories, and compiled a 6-4 record in five World Series. His finest campaign came in 1910 with a blister-

1912 E300 Plow's Candy – Chief Bender

chronologically came later, like 1914-1915 Cracker Jack. The source of the discrepancy rests in these large, sepia-toned treasures' virtual obscurity up until the 1960s. *Catalog* author Jefferson Burdick neglected to include them in the early editions of his master-work, simply because their stark rarity withheld the cards from his purview. Indeed, new exemplars have even been photographs of the period. Many of the game's highest-profile figures are pres-ent—Ty Cobb, Walter Johnson, Honus Wagner, Napoleon Lajoie, Christy Mathewson—along with lesser-known Hall of Famers like Fred Clarke, Roger Bresnahan, and Chief Bender. Born Charley Albert Bender of German and Chippewa descent, the prodigious right-hander was an idol to many ing 23-5 mark and 1.58 ERA, topped off by a no-hitter against the Cleveland Indians. Bender is also attributed with invention of the "nickel curve"—that ubiquitous component of modern pitching repertoires called the slider. Hail to the Chief!

Estimated Value: $2,000

TY COBB

TYRUS RAYMOND COBB
Champion Batsman, 1911

"Ty" Cobb, one of the greatest ball players of all time, is still a young man, having passed his 25th birthday in December, 1911. His first experience in organized ball was with the Augusta team in 1904, when he was not yet 18. He did not at first shine as a professional, and was farmed to Anniston, where he batted so hard that he was recalled, and in 1905 hit .326 for Augusta. Detroit then bought him, but in the fall of that year he only batted .240 for them in 41 games. Next year he got into the charmed .300 circle with an average of .320, and has since batted as follows: 1907—.350, 1908—.324, 1909—.377, 1910—385, 1911—.420. In 1911 he scored 147 runs in 146 games, made 248 hits, 47 doubles, 24 triples, 8 home runs, and stole 83 bases, all together the most remarkable work ever done by a player in a full season. He is so very fast on the bases that he sometimes seems reckless, but the records show that he reaches the objective base safely more often than not.

FREE WITH
MINERS EXTRA
SMOKING TOBACCO.

SERIES OF CHAMPIONS
25 DESIGNS

FACTORY N2 DIST. MO.

CORONA OF GOLDen sunset, azure horizon, and fertile grass radiates around the Detroit Tigers' wunderkind, with his collared, three-quarter-sleeve uniform and determined

biography aptly praises, "*In 1911 he scored 147 runs in 146 games, made 248 hits, 47 doubles, 24 triples, 8 home runs, and stole 83 bases, all together the most remarkable work ever done by a player in a full season. He is so very fast*

ly before the rookie outfielder reported to Detroit for the 1905 season. His father, suspecting Cobb's mother of infidelity, stealthily sidled up outside their bedroom window one night after arriving home. He sought to catch his

1912 T227 Miners Extra
"Series of Champions" — Ty Cobb

countenance. The gorgeous rendering hails from a quartet of baseball subjects within the 25-card "Series of Champions" set produced by tobacco companies Honest Long Cut and Miners Extra. Ty Cobb was fresh off his banner year, for which the reverse-side

on the bases that he sometimes seems reckless, but the records show that he reaches the objective base safely more often than not." Much is made of Cobb's cutthroat tenacity, though the sources of his inner fury sometimes go unmentioned. One root cause took place short-

wife having an affair and so, cautiously, gazed into the room. Cobb's mother mistook her husband for a burglar and shot him dead. Thus began Ty Cobb's major-league career.
Estimated Value: $5,000

"CLEVELAND AMERICANS" was card shorthand for the *Cleveland* ballclub of the *American* League. The squad's actual name in 1913, two years prior to becoming the PC-problematic "Indians"

seated second from the right, was the first and only major-league player to die as a result of an on-field accident, the victim of an errant Carl Mays fastball on August 16, 1920. The ball rebounded off Chapman's head with such force

of 1914-15. Fatima issued its cigarettes both with team images (T200) and individual-player images (T222), the former also produced as redeemable oversized premiums according to the quaint explanation on each card's

1913 T200 Fatima Team Card —
Cleveland Americans

of today, was the Cleveland Naps—for franchise player Napoleon Lajoie. Lajoie arrived in Ohio at the outset of 1902 after six stellar campaigns in Philadelphia. Within a season, the

that Yankees hurler Mays, under the impression it had hit his bat, scooped up the grounder and slung it to first baseman Wally Pipp for the apparent first out of the inning. But Chapman still lay

reverse:

"On receipt of 40 'FATIMA' Cigarette coupons, we will send you an enlarged copy (size 13 x 21) of this picture (without advertising) or of any other picture in

"Naps" moniker was born. By 1913, the year of this Fatima-issued insert, Lajoie was no longer his team's main draw. Shoeless Joe Jackson had landed in Cleveland following a stint in Philly as well. From 1911 to 1913, Jackson batted .408, .395, and .373 to Lajoie's none-too-shabby .365, .368, and .335. The two pose here in opposite corners, Jackson at top left and Lajoie lower right, but there is yet another noteworthy figure. Shortstop Ray Chapman,

on the ground near home plate. With the help of teammates, he was able to stand and walk a brief stretch before crumpling to the ground, losing consciousness, and finally dying 12 hours later in a New York City hospital. Back in 1913, Chapman's death and Shoeless Joe's banishment from baseball naturally were still unforeseen events. The year was a dry spell between the tobacco-card bonanza of 1909-11 and the Cracker Jack candy-card proliferation

this series (National League and American League teams). This picture is mounted, and ready for framing. Write plainly your name and address, stating picture desired."

These giant, seldom-encountered versions—especially that of the Cleveland Naps—are even more hotly pursued by hobbyists than the Fatima team cards themselves.
Estimated Value: $2,500

AT FIRST GLANCE, THIS might seem to be an advertisement for jockstraps. But a second look reveals that Joe Tinker is actually perched atop an elastic, clasped contrivance for holding card should—perish the thought!—reach the hands of unruly young collectors). Joining the ever-popular Tinker were Joe Jackson, Tris Speaker, Ty Cobb, Burt Shotton, Johnny Evers, Rabbit Maranville, Larry Doyle, Frank text: a checklist, career statistics, retail instructions, a corporate logo, and a sales pitch: "The good dreamer wants garter quality in keeping with the good quality of his Underwear and Hosiery. His socks cost 50 cents or more, and

1914 H813 Boston Garter #4 — Joe Tinker

up a fashionable man's socks: the garter. In 1914, Boston Garter issued twelve of these oversized window cards free of charge to retail outlets. Additional cards could be acquired by mail, so long as any incoming request proved its commercial intent by appearing "on business stationery" (lest the "Home Run" Baker, Ed Konetchy, Walter Johnson, and Buck Herzog. At approximately 4" x 8", Boston Garters are among the largest cards represented in this book, and their unwieldy dimensions factor significantly in the set's susceptibility to damage. Each item's reverse is chock-a-block with he'll buy the Pad Boston Garter at 50 cents." If only the buyers and sellers had known then what we know now—that the optimum value was not in the garters, but the overlooked and oft-discarded display cards.

Estimated Value: $5,000

"SHOELESS JOE" JACKSON IS, OF course, irrevocably tied to the Chicago White Sox, for it was his tenure with the Pale Hose that begat Jackson's lifetime banishment from baseball. But the native of Greenville, South Carolina, also played

Jackson's swing. Several years later in 1914, Cracker Jack showcased Shoeless Joe's follow-through by embellishing a photographic image taken by premier baseball cameraman Charles M. Conlon. Jackson's white jersey crackles against the issue's trademark tomato-red back-

1914 E145-1 Cracker Jack #103 — Joe Jackson

several seasons with the Cleveland Naps—here dubbed the Cleveland Americans for their jun-ior-circuit affiliation—and began his career with Connie Mack's Philadelphia Athletics. Jackson was an acclaimed phenom with his local semi-

ground. Amazingly, this artistic piece and its kin were distributed as hidden prizes in boxes of the all-American concession, without any protec-tion whatsoever in terms of a paper sleeve or plastic cover. As a result, most surviving cards

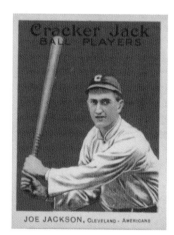

pro ballclub when Manager Mack came knock-ing with a major-league contract. So began a two-year saga wherein the illiterate country boy would play a brief stint in Philadelphia, then, daunted by the big city and ribbed by his street-savvy teammates, suddenly retreat to Greenville without warning. Eventually, in 1911, Mack tired of the cat-and-mouse charade, and Jackson found a happier home farther west in Cleveland. He batted .408 in his first full season and, to Ty Cobb's chagrin, earned a reputation as the game's greatest natural hitter, with even Babe Ruth acknowledging that he emulated

from the production show extensive damage due to the sugar-coated confection. Cracker Jack changed its methods the following year, making its 1915 offering—similar to its prede-cessor in design, numbering and subjects—redeemable by mail with proof of purchase. Jackson's more prevalent, less condition-sensi-tive 1915 card again has the fleet-footed out-fielder playing for the Cleveland Naps, even though he and his fate were dealt to the White Sox in August of that year.
Estimated Value: $5,000

Christopher Mathewson, pitcher of the
New York National League team, was born
in Factoryville, Pa., August 12, 1878. He
first attracted attention by his work for the
Keystone Academy team of Factoryville.
In 1897 he played with the Y. M. C. A. team
of Scranton, and the next year he pitched
for Bucknell College. He became a professional in 1899, as a member of the Hones-
dale, Pa., team. In 1900 Mathewson joined
the Giants.

This is one of a series of colored pictures
of famous Ball Players and Managers given
Free with Cracker Jack, "The Famous Pop-
corn Confection," one card in each package.
Our first issue is 15,000,000 pictures. Com-
plete set has 144 pictures of Stars in the
American, National and Federal Leagues.
RUECKHEIM BROS. & ECKSTEIN
Brooklyn, N. Y.   Chicago, Ill.

CRACKER JACK
BALL PLAYERS
MATHEWSON, NEW YORK - NATIONALS

TO UNEARTH CHRISTY Mathewson from the mounds of caramel-coated peanuts and popcorn was the dream of most any lad of the mid-1910s. In this horizontal action pose, Mathewson's out-

campaign of 20 or more wins, with a 24-13 showing that included 29 complete games. The following year, Cracker Jack offered its "insert" prizes as mail-in redemptions, a strategy that resulted in cleaner, more widely available cards

of players received different depictions—in Matty's case, a dignified quarter-turn portrait. Aesthetically, each portrayal has its merits. In terms of desirability, however, the forerunner is of paramount importance due to the

1914 E145-1 Cracker Jack #88 — Christy Mathewson

stretched arm appears ready to place the stitched orb directly into the catcher's mitt, which, given Matty's pinpoint accuracy, is not so far from the truth. In 1914, he posted his twelfth consecutive

that had never come into contact with the company's sticky confection. Most of the 1915 Cracker Jacks are identical to their corresponding item in the preceding production, but a small number

prohibitive scarcity of the 1914 issue in general and Mathewson's entry in particular.
Estimated Value: $25,000

THERE ARE TWO DIS-
tinct versions of these intriguing cards, which were sold with
a type of candy bar dubbed "Texas

reverse, and the scarcer, smaller,
glossier Type 2's are blank-backed.
Both varieties showcase the player's
full-size image with a legend denoting

the Type 2's. A 36-7 record, 29 complete games, 11 shutouts, 243 strikeouts and a 1.14 ERA added up to MVP
hardware and pitching's Triple Crown

1914 E224 Texas Tommy Type 2 —
Walter Johnson

Tommy" after the popular dance of the
same name. The more prevalent Type
1's are marked "Texas Tommy" on the

surname and affiliation. Walter
Johnson was on the heels of his best
big-league campaign when he landed in

for the era's preeminent moundsman,
the mighty "Big Train."
Estimated Value: $10,000

Babe Ruth, the pitcher.

RUTH
PITCHER
INTERNATIONAL
LEAGUE BALTO.

COMPLIMENTS OF
BALTIMORE
INTERNATIONAL LEAGUE
1914   When and Where the   1914
Orioles Play.

Card Photos Courtesy of Professional Sports Authenticator (PSA)

HERE IS THE BEST *PRE-* rookie card in the hobby. Minor-leaguer George Herman Ruth, an unknown pitcher out of St. Mary's Industrial School for Boys, stands tall in his new uniform for the Baltimore Orioles of the International League. On his right hand, a glove; on his face, an expression of bewildered naïveté. *The Baltimore News* selected Ruth as a subject for the simple reason that the daily was publishing a set with combatants from the city's two ball-clubs: the Orioles and the Federal League's Terrapins. Fewer than 10 copies of the card are thought to exist due to the issue's obscurity, fragile stock, and limited, regional market. One specimen in mid-grade recently realized more than $240,000 at auction. Lettered on the reverse is the Orioles' playing schedule, below the header "Compliments of Baltimore International League" (substituted on some of its brethren with "Read the Baltimore News"). Ruth's bright future—and that of the national pastime he would champion, raising it overhead as Atlas held up the world—has its inception with this transcendent rarity, depicting the future legend with those boyish features that gave rise to his singular nickname, "Babe."
Estimated Value: $200,000

1914 BALTIMORE NEWS — BABE RUTH

AS BEANTOWN FANS are painfully aware, before Babe started clobbering opposing pitchers in his familiar Yankee pinstripes, the Sultan of Swat was a moundsman himself—the ace of respond? By shipping their wonder boy to the New York Yankees in exchange for $100,000 and a misfortune to be named later. The BoSox wouldn't win their next championship until 2004, the 85th anniversary of the so-called subscribers, the 200-card set was obtainable by mail and its subjects bore a *Sporting News* reverse or had blank backs. Companies such as Famous and Barr clothiers also special-ordered copies with their advertisements on the

1916 M101-5 Sporting News #151 — Babe Ruth

the Boston Red Sox pitching staff. Ruth authored 65 wins, 16 shutouts, and a 2.07 ERA in his first three full seasons (1915-1917), as he gradually drew more and more attention for his batting "Curse of the Bambino," despite such talented players as Ted Williams, Carl Yastrzemski, and Wade Boggs, the last of whom would leave the Red Sox to hoist a championship trophy with, who reverse. The blank-backed variety shows up most often on this, the Babe's cherished rookie card. In all of baseball photography, there are few sights as visually arresting as a young, svelte

BABE RUTH
P.—Boston Red Sox
151

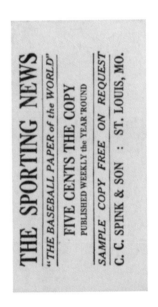

prowess. By 1919, the dominant southpaw's contributions had evolved to only 17 pitching appearances against 111 games played in the outfield. Babe hit .322 with 114 RBI and an unprecedented 29 home runs that year, while still logging a respectable 9-5 record and 2.97 ERA. How did the team's executives else, the winningest franchise in baseball history, the Yankees. Alas, if only the Boston brass had taken a cue from *The Sporting News*. Publisher J.G. Taylor Spink's "Bible of Baseball" saw Ruth's potential from the very start, featuring the as-yet-unproven pitcher in its 1916 series of photographic premiums. For Babe Ruth completing his delivery as a Red Sox hurler. The home run records, the "called shot," the fortune and fame, "The House That Ruth Built," these bedrocks of baseball lore have yet to be born.
Estimated Value: $25,000

JIM THORPE
R. F.—New York Giants
176

SOMETHING ABOUT JIM Thorpe's pose on this card calls to mind a comic-book superhero. It is as if Thorpe has just broken out of chains padlocked by his arch-enemy, and now pauses for the requi-call him Batman. But Superman better suits his reputation. The American-Indian hailed as "The Greatest Athlete of the 20th Century" played six major-league seasons (1913-1915, 1917-1919), while also starring for football's that were later revoked because the Olympian's previous play on semi-pro baseball teams negated his declared status as an amateur athlete). Thorpe averaged about 50 games per year in the majors, compiling a lifetime batting

1916 M101-5 Sporting News #176 — Jim Thorpe

site full-length shot of his brawny physique before soaring off to save humanity in the nick of time. Judging by his Gotham locale and his hitting lumber—which looks like a piece of kindling in Thorpe's powerful grip—one might Canton Bulldogs. His specialty, though, was track and field. At the 1912 Olympics in Stockholm, Thorpe amazed spectators and trounced competitors with gold-medal performances in the decathlon and pentathlon (medals mark of .252. His two best-known base-ball cards are a minor-league appearance in the long-running Zeenut series and this Man-of-Steel depiction produced by *The Sporting News*.
Estimated Value: $5,000

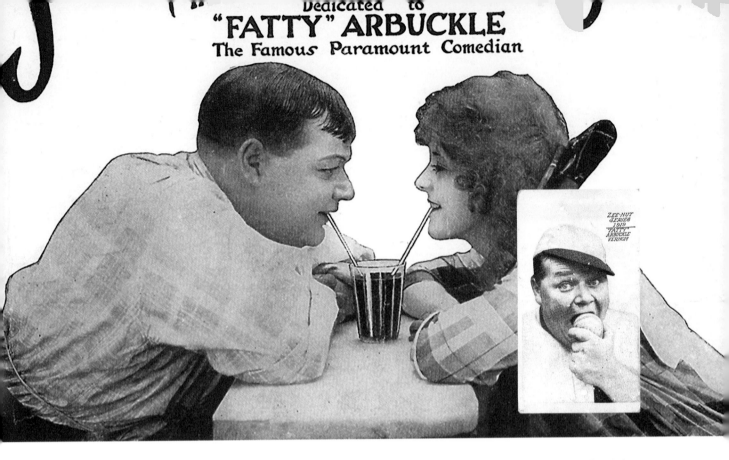

THE ONLY HOLLYWOOD star of his generation to occupy baseball cardboard, Roscoe "Fatty" Arbuckle garnered his cameo as a team owner in the Pacific Coast League (PCL). He bought a stake in the becoming one of the most popular and highest-paid actors in Tinseltown. Seeing him chomp into a baseball as if it were an apple, his eyes wide with child-like wonder, would have induced a fit of laughter in any movie-going consumer possibly having funded an illegal abortion for her, Arbuckle became a prime suspect in the murder investigation and subsequent court trial—a media bonanza perhaps best compared in modern times to the O.J. Simpson case. Like

1919 E137 ZEENUT PCL – FATTY ARBUCKLE

Vernon Tigers organization prior to the 1919 season—the first of the Tigers' two consecutive PCL-championship years. Beyond success, his presence also brought glamour to the franchise: Tom Mix and Buster Keaton attended Opening Day festivities. At the time, everything Arbuckle touched turned to gold. He was a silent-film sensation, made famous by his slapstick antics in the *Keystone Kops* film series and then of Zeenut candy. A few years later, however, this whimsical card of the Babe Ruth look-alike might have provoked the same buyer to paroxysms of anger. Never has a celebrity plummeted from such great heights as Arbuckle did following the death of actress Virginia Rappe, who suffered a ruptured bladder after a party in 1921 with the portly comedian and friends. Implicated of sexually assaulting the young woman, or Simpson, Arbuckle was acquitted in court but nonetheless remained guilty in the eyes of the public. Blacklisted by production studios and demonized by critics, he turned increasingly to alcohol and died of a heart attack on June 29, 1933. Keaton, whose defense of Arbuckle's innocence had never flagged, insisted the cause of death was a broken heart.

Estimated Value: $500

Eddie Collins (left) and Johnny Evers.

S TRIP CARDS. TO SOME, they are the hobby's ugly duckling; to others, an unlikely swan. Anonymously produced in the 1920s, during the lull between the second and third waves of major baseball-card sets, the earliest examples were Ruth. Hall of Fame second baseman Eddie Collins managed to elude such a fate. His depiction in 1923's 60-subject, W515-1 release is subdued, attractive even, overlooking the unusual touch of his pants matching the color Chicago White Sox. It was a tenure in which he saw eight of his Pale Hose teammates banished from baseball for throwing the 1919 World Series. (He, himself, batted a measly .226 in the series.) Ranked in the Top 10 for total

1923 W515-1 Strip Card #58 — Eddie Collins

card sets, the earliest examples were sold in 10-card strips. Consumers cut the strips by hand with scissors, a practice which, combined with the issues' inexpensive paper stock, has largely resulted in abysmal condition. Adding insult to injury, strip cards tend to consist of amateurish, almost grotesque illustrations—especially those of Babe of his bat. Collins was then in the second phase of his acclaimed 25-year career. After starring in Connie Mack's famously high-paid "$100,000 Infield"—with fellow Philadelphia Athletics Stuffy McInnis at first, Jack Barry at shortstop, and Frank "Home Run" Baker at third—Collins was now in the midst of twelve seasons with the hits with 3,315, Collins compiled a lifetime .333 mark at the plate yet, due in no small part to Ty Cobb, never won a batting title. Conversely, while Cobb was unable to fulfill his own championship dreams, Collins four times enjoyed the thrill of October glory. *Estimated Value: $100*

T HIS IS LOU GEHRIG'S rookie card. Considering that many hobbyists have a Pavlovian reaction upon hearing "Iron Horse" or "rookie" in separate contexts, the combination of the two in one outstanding collectible should be cause for jubilation. Dueling auction paddles should elevate the gavel-pounded winning bid to upwards of six figures. Right? In actuality, Gehrig's freshman picture receives little attention compared to his sought-after gum cards of the 1930s. It is a case of guilt by association. *All* exhibit cards are underestimated and undervalued. They are the Rodney Dangerfield of the card-col-

lecting circuit. Disseminated in penny arcades and amusement parks, "exhibits" were popularized by Chicago's Exhibit Supply Company. The firm manufactured and distributed free-standing machines that shared three integral features: a selection of high-profile players' cards behind glass to tantalize prospective buyers with what could be; a coin slot for the cold, hard change; and a chute from which inevitably emerged lesser-known players than the ones displayed above. Drat! But, like grownups in casinos, few youngsters could resist the temptation to play again and again, praying for the almighty jackpot. Throughout the base-

ball-card industry's highs and lows from the 1920s to 1960s—the fits, starts, fizzles, and evolutions—exhibits remained a singular constant. They began with annual sets and concluded with long-running issues like 1939-46 Salutation

1925 Exhibit Card — Lou Gehrig

(82 cards) and 1947-66 (336 cards). Gehrig's debut belongs to Exhibit Supply Company's 1925 edition of 128 subjects. On June 2nd of that year, the Yankees prospect out of Columbia University filled in at first base for starter Wally Pipp, an individual whose name is now synonymous with poor timing. Gehrig would hold the starting job for his next 2,130 straight games. *Estimated Value: $2,500*

N EVER WAS THERE AN ATHLETE MORE
suited for ice-cream endorsement than
Babe Ruth. His appetite was legendary.
Ruth downed hamburgers and hot dogs like a National
Eating Champion, then topped off his feasts with mouth-
watering desserts such as, well, Fro-joy Ice Cream. In

1928 F52 FRO-JOY
ICE CREAM #4 —
BABE RUTH

August of 1928, as part of its "Fro-joy Cone Week" promotion, the company produced six small cards of the
Bambino in a variety of depictions—two actions scenes,
two posed pictures, a bust-length portrait, and a close-up
shot of his batting grip. The most distinctive image cap-

**When The
"Babe" Comes
Home**

Feet first, the "Babe"
beats the ball to the
home plate by inches.
He doesn't have to
do this often. Usu-
ally he "dog trots"
around after a circuit
smash. But when the
occasion arises, the
"Big Bat Boy", in
spite of his bulk, can
run bases with the
best of them.

tures Ruth in a dynamic feet-first slide. Enumerated on the
back are a host of health benefits ("Fro-joy Ice Cream, if
eaten daily, builds strong bodies and sound teeth and
bones. Its 'Youth Units' create energy and vigor") and an
invitation for mail-in submissions of the sextet in exchange
for an oversized, facsimile-signed photographic premium
of Ruth. Modern-day collectors are often wary of Fro-joy
cards—and the uncut six-card sheet that accompanied
Ruth's premium photo as part of the redemption
process—because there are numerous reproductions
circulating in the hobby.
Estimated Value: $250

"Babe" Ruth says:—
"I understand your Fro-joy Ice Cream
is Chock-full of Youth Units and that Fro-joy
Cones are pure and wholesome. I want to
give each one of these thousand orphan
boys a Fro-joy Cone filled to the brim with
Fro-joy Ice Cream"   "Babe" Ruth

Excerpt from a letter
from "Babe Ruth order-
ing Fro-joy for his or-
phan boy guests at
his Boston baseball
party.

"Fro-joy"
ICE
CREAM
CONES
Chock-full of
"Youth Units!"

An extremely rare Fro-Joy
advertising counter card.

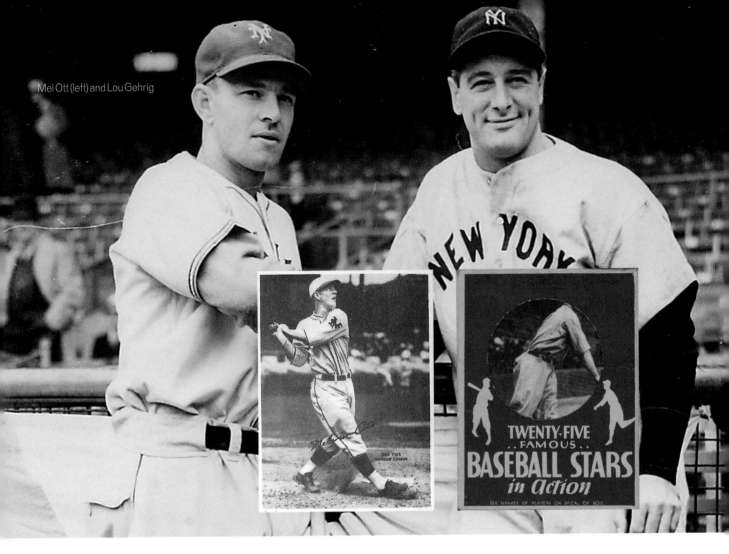

Mel Ott (left) and Lou Gehrig

"MASTER MELVIN" gazed skyward often in his breakout season of 1929. The short, stocky right fielder with the high-leg-kick swing emanates from a set of 101 facsimile-signed picture cards produced by Kashin Publications. Highlighted by Ott and his fellow future "500 Home Run Club" members Jimmie Foxx and Babe season career with the New York Giants, first under the managerial tenures of John McGraw and Bill Terry and later as the team's player/manager. He hung up his cleats in 1947 with

1929 R316 Kashin Publications — Mel Ott

launched a career-best 42 home runs to go along with 151 RBI, 138 runs, 113 walks (including six in a doubleheader!), 37 doubles, a .328 average, and a .635 slugging percentage. All that at just 20 years old. This postcard-size action shot Ruth (who already had his eye on 600), the blank-backed issue came in "viewer boxes" of 25 cards apiece. A circular window on the box-front zeroed in on the players from the waist up. Ultimately, Ott played his entire 22- what was then the National League's most prolific long-ball total: 511. Autograph collectors recognize Ott, who died in 1958, as one of the most difficult signatures of any 500-home-run hitter. *Estimated Value: $100*

*I*T WAS THE BEST OF SETS, IT was the worst of sets. It was a set of widespread appeal and demand, it was a set that wrought turmoil, deception, and betrayal. At first, everything seemed rosy. The pixilated portraits of U.S. Caramel's "Famous Athletes" production helped quench a card drought that youngsters had bemoaned since the rationed run-up to the First World War. Thanks in large part

case of outright chicanery. **EXHIBIT A**: On the reverse of each R328 card resides the protocol for redemption, which states, "*This is one of a series of famous athletes numbered from 1 to 32. Return a complete set and receive a league BASEBALL, value $1.00, or return three complete sets and receive a FIELDER'S GLOVE, value $3.00 (state whether left or right handed). Your pictures will be returned with the gifts.*"

set, making Lindstrom an easy target whose unavailability only the most scrupulous set-builders would notice. **EXHIBIT E**: U.S. Caramel produced a subsequent gallery of American Presidents and pulled the same stunt, short-printing William McKinley (a White House martyr, no less!) to avoid bestowing upon buyers the promised, redeemable prize of a one-pound box of chocolates—thus lending credence to

1932 R328 U.S. Caramel #16 — "Lindy" Lindstrom

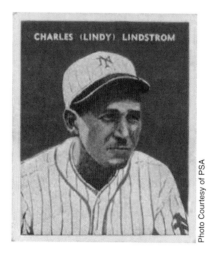

CHARLES (LINDY) LINDSTROM

Photo Courtesy of PSA

to the Boston-based confection firm and its competitor Goudey Gum Company, baseball cards were back in full force—less one, that is. *Both* producers managed to omit a key component of their sets. For Goudey, history tells us that the absence of #106 Nap Lajoie resulted from negligence; for U.S. Caramel's mishap regarding #16 Charles "Lindy" Lindstrom (a.k.a. Freddy Lindstrom), the record shows a

EXHIBIT B: Of the 27 ballplayers and five other athletes represented, many dozens or even hundreds of copies exist for numbers 1 to 15 and 17 to 32, including high-profile stars the likes of Babe Ruth and Ty Cobb. **EXHIBIT C**: The above #16 is one of a mere two specimens extant. **EXHIBIT D**: Mr. Lindstrom's statistics and popularity through the early 1930s paled in comparison to the Ruths and Cobbs of the

Forrest Gump's maxim on the subject, "You never know what you're gonna get." Alas, very few cavity-ridden consumers, no matter how many sweets they bought, ever completed the quests and received their well-earned baseball, fielder's glove, or chocolates. Fortunately, the true prizes were (and still are) the cards themselves.
Estimated Value: $75,000

*L*IKE THOSE OF U.S. Caramel, the 32 portraits in gum producer George C. Miller & Company's one-and-only foray into cards were distributed as a means to an end. Anyone who assembled and redeemed the entire set would, according to each card's reverse, "receive FREE OF CHARGE, your choice of Fielder's Mit [sic], regulation American or National League Baseball or 1

era. Naturally, cards that were never submitted remained safely intact. The roster included two figures from each of the 16 major-league teams, including Bill Dickey, Lefty Grove, Joe Cronin, Charlie Gehringer, Rabbit Maranville, Mel Ott, and both Waner brothers. Only one player, Ivy Andrews, is almost invariably cancelled, with only a few examples ever seen of his as-issued, full-size cards. Why the anomaly? In a

He was little known enough that his absence would not be mourned (or even observed) except by the most fervent young collector. And, perhaps more significantly, although Andrews is pictured as a New York Yankee, he had

1933 R300 George C. Miller & Co. — Ivy Andrews

recently joined the pitching stable of the Boston Red Sox—Miller & Co.'s hometown team. Were it not for the sales gimmick and harsh cancellations, this pretty release might have attained

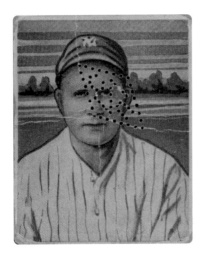 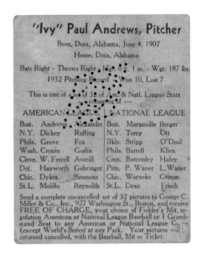

Grandstand Seat to any American or National League Game (except World's Series) at any Park." In addition to the glove, ball, or ticket, winners were also sent back their card submissions— but in cancelled form to dissuade re-entry. Most were missing their lower one-third portion, resulting in a small, odd-shaped versions of their former glory; others were punched with a perforation pattern, like bank checks of the

disreputable tactic mimicking U.S. Caramel's scheme of the previous year, George C. Miller & Co. intentionally short-printed Andrews so as to undermine the quest for set completion—in other words, to save money on the redemption prizes. Being the most crucial acquisition, Andrews' cards were inevitably exchanged and cancelled. The third-year hurler dubbed "Poison" seems, in retrospect, an obvious choice.

a status on par with the more widely released Goudey cards of the same year. Instead, the R300 George C. Millers go down in hobby history as an esoteric edition of amputations and oddities, adored by collectors who are willing to forsake pristine condition for intriguing, conspiratorial circumstances. *Estimated Value: $20,000*

THE GOUDEY GUM COMPANY did everything right in its rookie year of card production, breaking ground with gorgeous portraits, resplendent hues, star power, and in-depth player information. They only forgot one teensy-weensy detail: #106. sheets. Anyone who had written a complaint received an apologetic response letter, along with a copy of the elusive, freshly minted card that had started the whole uproar. No other copies were released to the public. And so, a long-ago boondoggle led to a boon for modern-

1933 R319 Goudey #106 — Napoleon Lajoie

Napoleon Lajoie simply never made it to the printing press. Among Goudey's tender-aged clientele, most youngsters probably noticed the gaffe only if they were trying to assemble an entire set. Sadly, no matter how many packs of day collectors, whose greatest love is a rarity with a compelling back-story. In that mold, Honus Wagner's T206 reigns supreme, with Nap Lajoie running a distant second. The French-Canadian Lajoie, who had retired from

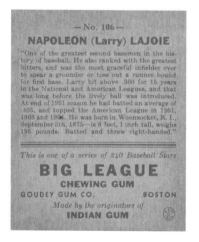

cards were bought and riffled through, not a single one would ever unveil the magic missing number. When enough childhood tears were shed, parents began writing letters to the manufacturer, demanding an explanation for what seemed fraudulent advertising and corrupt marketing. Goudey knew the old adage about customers always being right—and never had it been more true. By this time, the firm was in the thick of creating its 1934 "Lou Gehrig Says" set, and company executives decided to avoid a public-relations nightmare by adding #106—Lajoie—to 1934's "high-number" production the game back in 1915, received his due honor in Goudey's issue a mere three seasons before earning induction to the Hall of Fame. The card's reverse hails the lifetime .339 batsman as, "One of the greatest second basemen in the history of baseball. He also ranked with the greatest hitters, and was the most graceful infielder ever to spear a grounder or toss out a runner bound for first base." On the card-front, Lajoie's lips are taut but his eyes and cheeks foretell a blossoming smile and, perhaps, a chuckle at Goudey's embarrassing error of omission.

Estimated Value: $50,000

GEORGE HERMAN
(BABE) RUTH

— No. 144 —
GEORGE HERMAN (BABE) RUTH
NEW YORK YANKEES
Cost Red Sox less than $3,000 in 1914, but New
York Yankees paid about $125,000 for him six
years later. Stepped from industrial school in
Baltimore to minor league ball and went to big
league in less than a year.
   Was star pitcher for several years, but now plays
in outfield. Holds big league home run record, 60,
made in 1927. Led American League in batting in
1924. Last year batted .341 and hit 41 homers.
Is 39 years old, six feet, two inches tall and
weighs 210. Bats and throws left handed.

This is one of a series of 240 Baseball Stars
BIG LEAGUE
CHEWING GUM
GOUDEY GUM CO.   BOSTON
Made by the originators of
INDIAN GUM

BIG LEAGUE CHEWING GUM

O F THE MORE THAN 200 players depicted in Goudey's '33 set, nearly all are so honored once, a handful were deemed worthy of two representations, and the larger-than-life Bambino, Goudey—the first prominent company to disseminate their cards in packs of bubblegum instead of candy or tobacco—sought to be the vanguard of a new era in Ruthian collectibles. All four of the company's debut offerings are hobby throwback to a simpler time. Rather than show Ruth as the paunchy, fading 39-year-old he had become by 1933, Goudey presents him in his prime, hale as ever, his warm gaze transfixed on the viewer, exactly how we crave to remem-

1933 R319 Goudey #144 — Babe Ruth

never to be outdone, shines forth from *four* distinct cards: #'s 53, 144, 149, and 181. In all likelihood, Goudey was not simply promoting the set's biggest draw, but also compensating for the dearth of Ruth's cardboard cameos in the preceding years. The major manufacturers had taken a hiatus from World War I up until the early 1930's, and

favorites, yet this lush rendering, #144, holds sway. The uplifting design is a masterwork of the genre. It proffers vibrant hues, the slugger's sole "action" pose in the issue, and his only appearance in Yankee pinstripes. The quaint grandstand underscores a setting far removed from the capacity crowds and frenzied pace of New York City—a

ber him. Ruth's joy is immediately evident, and not because of the drinking, the ladies, and the fame that consumed his latter years, but merely because of the field, the bat, the uniform, the smell of new grass, and the sight of a well-struck horsehide sphere soaring over the distant outfield wall.
Estimated Value: $18,500

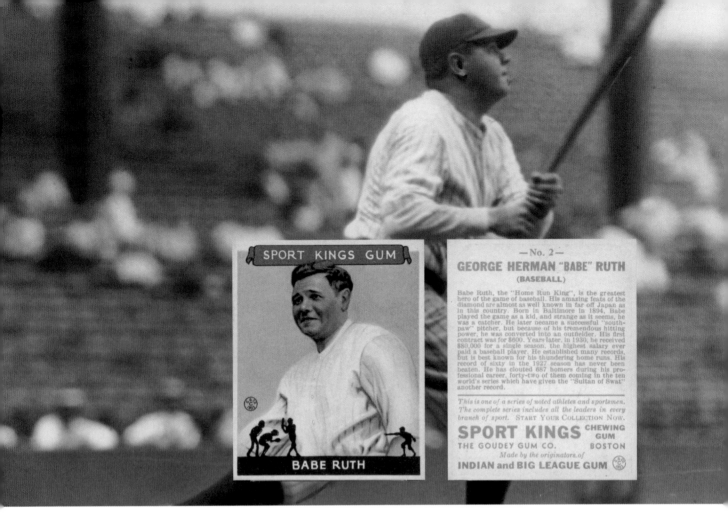

SPORT KINGS GUM

BABE RUTH

—No. 2—
GEORGE HERMAN "BABE" RUTH
(BASEBALL)

Babe Ruth, the "Home Run King", is the greatest hero of the game of baseball. His amazing feats of the diamond are almost as well known in far off Japan as in this country. Born in Baltimore in 1894, Babe played the game as a kid, and strange as it seems, he was a catcher. He later became a successful "southpaw" pitcher, but because of his tremendous hitting power, he was converted into an outfielder. His first contract was for $600. Years later, in 1930, he received $80,000 for a single season, the highest salary ever paid a baseball player. He established many records, but is best known for his thundering home runs. His record of sixty in the 1927 season has never been beaten. He has clouted 687 homers during his professional career, forty-two of them coming in the ten world's series which have given the "Sultan of Swat" another record.

This is one of a series of noted athletes and sportsmen. The complete series includes all the leaders in every branch of sport. START YOUR COLLECTION NOW.

SPORT KINGS CHEWING GUM
THE GOUDEY GUM CO.   BOSTON
Made by the originators of
INDIAN and BIG LEAGUE GUM

WHAT DISTINGUISH-es the 48-card Sport Kings set from nearly all other gum-card collectibles is its multi-sport content. Diamond royalty Babe Ruth, Ty Cobb, and Carl Hubbell hob-nob with links legends Bobby Jones and Walter Hagen, billiards virtuoso Willie Hoppe, pugilists Jack Dempsey and Max Baer, gridiron stars Red Grange and Knute Rockne, athletes extraordinaire Jim Thorpe and Babe Didrikson (one of two "queens" among Goudey's sovereigns), and many more standouts whose names are less heralded now than they were three-quarters of a century ago. Ruth's portrait succeeds in encapsulating his affable, fun-loving nature and his powerful physique. In fact, were it not for the instant name and face recognition or the silhouetted baseball scene, one might mistake Ruth for a football great, perhaps clutching a pigskin below the bottom border. Flip the card over and a player biography crowns Ruth the monarch of his sport's sluggers, and possibly of the entire world: "Babe Ruth, the 'Home Run King', is the greatest hero of the game of baseball. His amazing feats of the diamond are almost as well known in far off Japan as in this country." Long live His Majesty, King Ruth.
Estimated Value: $27,500

1933 R338 GOUDEY SPORT KINGS #2 — BABE RUTH

*T*HAT GOUDEY-DOMIN-ated "Golden Age" of the early 1930s also gave rise to a host of competitors for the gum-card crown. One such hopeful was Tattoo Orbit, an off-shoot of the Wrigley Company. The due to Phillip K. Wrigley's ownership of the ballclub), and it is possible that Tattoo Orbits were predominately sold in those surrounding Midwestern markets. Rogers Hornsby, whose impeccable career had then reached its down-

1933 R305 Tattoo Orbit — Rogers Hornsby

space-age name and avant-garde color scheme equated to 60 cards total, which were unusual for the period because of their small physical size, their thin, easily damaged paper stock, and their lack of a numbering system. A substantial portion of the set emphasized players from the St. Louis Cardinals and Chicago Cubs (the latter swing, was a mainstay of the region. "Rajah" had played for the Cubs from 1929 to 1932, then briefly returned to the Cardinals (his former team for 12 seasons) in 1933, before finishing out that year and the next four with the junior circuit's St. Louis Browns. Hornsby's rendering in the Ruth-and-Gehrig-less Tattoo Orbit issue joins three other subjects—Bump Hadley, Ivy Andrews, and George Blaeholder—as a quartet of inordinately tough acquisitions. Other notables in the set include Jimmie Foxx, Lefty Grove, and Dizzy Dean.

Estimated Value: $1,500

---

*T*HE DELONG GUM Company was a cardboard "one-hit wonder." Its visionary, 24-subject set coincided with the Goudey Gum Company's 239-card debut, an issue that was better financed illustrated stadium scene and robin's-egg blue sky. DeLong's designers seized on the figures' larger-than-life status, turning abstract metaphor into reality. One obstacle to the set's success was the absence of Babe Ruth,

LOU GEHRIG
NEW YORK YANKEES

1933 R333 DeLong #7 — Lou Gehrig

and more widely disseminated. Simply put, Goudey flourished and DeLong perished. Still, the firm's limited print runs and avant-garde graphics have had hobbyists "DeLonging" for them ever since. Each card in the superstar-studded production flaunts a Brobdingnagian ballplayer against an especially in light of Goudey's quartet of Ruthian renderings. Consequently, Lou Gehrig was the primary draw—and has sustained that role to this day. This artistic creation is one of Gehrig's most seldom-encountered cards and, in many eyes, his best. If ever there was a competitor whose very presence and integrity transcended the game itself, it was "The Pride of the Yankees," Lou Gehrig.

Estimated Value: $26,000

LOU GEHRIG LIVED UNDER Babe Ruth's looming shadow—a solar eclipse, really—for the first decade of his career. In 1934, Gehrig stepped into the light. While Babe endured a lackluster final season tion—and offered center stage to Gehrig. The "Iron Horse" laid claim to two different cards, but, more importantly, Goudey based their entire design on Gehrig's popularity. Numbers 1 through 72 of the 96-card set were me..." Gehrig's words drip with tragic irony, of course, since his career would soon draw to a close, "Fortune" being anything but kind. Within a few short years, baseball's living embodiment of strength and vigor would be too enfee-

1934 R320 Goudey #37 — Lou Gehrig

in Yankee pinstripes, his humble teammate flourished on the diamond. Gehrig won the A.L Triple Crown with a .363 batting average, a career-high 49 home runs, and 165 RBI. On cardboard, the passing of the torch was even more apparent. The Goudey Gum Company's sophomore effort omitted Ruth—the previous year's main attrac- anchored by a "Lou Gehrig Says" facsimile-signature banner complete with head shot. On the reverse, the All-Star first baseman provided color commentary for each player. In his own case, on the back of this card #37, he notes, "I love the game of baseball and hope to be in there batting them out for many years to come. Fortune has been kind to bled to take the field, a victim of the disease that now bears his name. On the card-front, Gehrig's fate seems an impossibility. He is the picture of health in those halcyon days of 1934, leaving us with the indelible image of his charming smile, warm expression, uncommon talent, and passion for life.

Estimated Value: $11,500

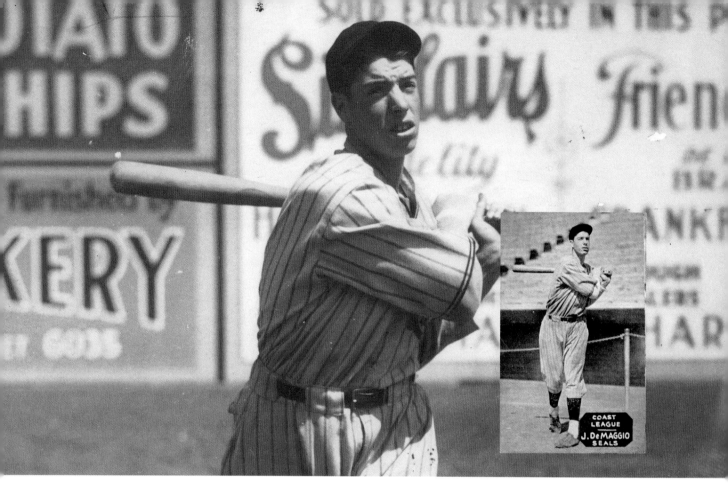

*T*HREE YEARS WITH THE San Francisco Seals of the Pacific Coast League (PCL) demonstrated what could be expected from Joseph Paul DiMaggio in the majors: high-octane statistics, team route to a postseason PCL title. He debuted on a pair of photographic, pre-rookie cards during that time, first, in the batting shot featured above, and second, in a throwing pose the following year (his name was misspelled on both 1880s. Zeenut highlights included Jim Thorpe, Claude "Lefty" Williams, Buck Weaver, Mickey Cochrane, Tony Lazzeri, and the Waner and DiMaggio brothers. A large majority of the cards were printed with perforated coupon tabs along

1934 E137 Zeenut PCL — Joe DiMaggio

championships, and, yes, hitting streaks. In 1933, his first full campaign in the PCL, DiMaggio batted safely in 61 straight games (five more, of course, than his acclaimed run with the Yankees in 1941). Two seasons later as a Seal, while under contact with the Yankees, Joltin' Joe compiled a robust .398 average, 154 RBI, and 35 home runs en occasions, as it was for his brothers Vince and Dom as well). The Zeenut series, produced by the Collins-McCarthy Candy Company, documented the PCL from 1911 through 1938 and amounted to several thousands of different cards—as daunting a task for today's set-builders as the vexatious Old Judge issues of the late the bottom, nearly all of which were removed because they were, as advertised, "Good for valuable premiums." DiMaggio's appearances repre-sented the apex for Zeenuts, whose production came to a halt around the same time the Yankee Clipper's big-league career was taking flight.

Estimated Value: $5,000

ALL CARDS HAVE encouraged some form of mistreatment, be it rubber-banded safekeeping, thumb-tacked display, flipping, greasy-fingered handling, or captivity in bike across the player's ankles for the intended "pop-up" purpose. Countless Batter-Ups were abused, mangled, and sullied in like fashion, thus bequeathing future generations a paltry amount of high-end copies. Adding to the set's of excellence. Dean averaged 24 wins from 1932 to 1936 and, in 1934, led the famed "Gashouse Gang" to a championship on the strength of a 30-7 record, a 2.66 ERA, and a six-hit shutout in Game 7 of the World Series. Here, he

1934–1936 R318 BATTER–UP #64 — DIZZY DEAN

spokes for motorcycle sound effects. With National Chicle's "Batter-Up" creation, mistreatment was a prerequisite. Step One entailed punching out the perforated outline by pressing upwards from underneath the player. For Step Two, consumers awkwardly made a horizontal crease either along the width of the lower portion or simply challenges, its 192 members classify as 80 "low numbers" and 112 "high numbers," with the disparity in availability between the two segments being perhaps the most lopsided in the hobby pantheon. "Ol' Diz" belongs to the earlier, more prevalent crop, no doubt because the popular fireballer was in the thick of a remarkable 5-year burst completes his delivery in a pose rather reminiscent of the "Creation of Adam" fresco atop the Sistine Chapel. After Dean's career came to a sudden conclusion due to an arm injury, he embarked on a successful, though faux-pas-filled tenure as a St. Louis Cardinals broadcaster.
Estimated Value: $1,900

ABSENT FROM THE 1934 Goudey offering, Babe Ruth returned in 1935 for his cardboard curtain call...as a Boston Brave. New York Yankees owner Jacob Ruppert had finally different frontal designs that together constitute a complete set. Taking into account the reverse-side puzzle (in which each card-back displays a rectangular portion of a larger photograph, either of an individual player or team) whose record of 23 National League seasons held up for over a half century. Maranville captured a championship back in 1914 with the "Miracle Braves," and eventually returned to the ballclub in 1929. He and the Bambino spent

1935 R321 Goudey 4-in-1 "Puzzle" — Babe Ruth/Rabbit Maranville

squeezed Babe out of the Big Apple, first by enforcing an annual pay cut of his salary and then by denying Ruth his long-held dream of managing the team after his playing days were over. So expands the total to a "master set" of 114 front/back combinations. With regard to Ruth's counterparts: Brandt, a southpaw pitcher who won 121 games in 11 seasons, epitomized his twenty years in opposing leagues from the 1910s through 1930s, competing only once in postseason play: a four-game sweep by Ruth's Yankees over Maranville's St. Louis Cardinals at the

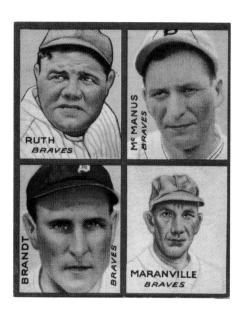

PICTURE 3 CARD A

Babe left the mighty Yankees and joined the lowly Braves. The Goudey Gum Company recycled his image from its 1933 release, card #181, and united him with teammates Rabbit Maranville, Marty McManus, and "Big Ed" Brandt. The foursome is one of 36 team's hapless performance in 1935 with a 5-19 record on the mound; McManus, who had actually retired the previous season, was a 15-season infielder with almost 2,000 lifetime hits; and Maranville, inducted into the Hall of Fame in 1954, was a 5-foot-5 shortstop 1928 World Series. Yet, in an unlikely turn of events, this physically contrasting pair shared their final big-league season together, before passing the torch to a new legion of baseball legends.

Estimated Value: $9,500

Posing together before the 1937 All-Star Game are (left to right) Lou Gehrig, Joe Cronin, Bill Dickey, Joe DiMaggio, Charlie Gehringer, Jimmie Foxx and Hank Greenberg.

DIAMOND STARS, No. 54

With a runner on first base, the baseman should stand just in front of the bag until the ball is pitched. As the pitcher throws, the first baseman will dash ten or fifteen feet off his bag to be in position for any hit that comes down his way. In taking throws from his pitcher to catch a runner off the base, the first sacker should put himself in perfect tagging position as the throw comes, so that he can make a sweeping tag in a single motion. A skillful man like Hank Greenberg of the Tigers, has mastered the trick of keeping his feet and legs out of range of the runner's spikes and using his long arms and height to make the tag.

Austin Lake   Boston American

HENRY GREENBERG. Born New York City, 34 years old; bats and throws right; 6 ft. 4 inches, 215 pounds. 1934 batting average .339; .321 in World's Series.

One of 240 major league players with playing tips
©1935 National Chicle Co. Cambridge, Mass. U.S.A.

"HANK" GREENBURG

I N THE BEGINNING, THERE were tobacco and candy cards. The early 1930s gave rise to that new contender for the cardboard crown: gum companies. Jefferson Burdick, author of the seminal either 1933, 1934, or 1935—on the reverse of the cards. Under these parameters, the 1934 issue contains 24 entries; 1935 delivers 84 (the first two dozen being updates from '34); and 1936 proffered another 36 (a dozen ("Greenburg"). The 24-year-old Greenberg won his first of two MVP awards that same year, as his Tigers notched a 4-2 World Series victory over the Chicago Cubs. Card #54 exemplifies the charismatic colors, sleek scenery,

1935 R327 DIAMOND STARS #54 VARIATION — HANK GREENBERG

American Card Catalog, christened gum cards with his "R" designation. For National Chicle's 1934-1936 "Diamond Stars" series, Burdick categorized all three editions of the three-year production as R327. Purists, however, point out that the sets are in fact individually distinguishable by virtue of the previous year's statistics—from being reprint subjects with '35 statistics, and the last 12 cards having reverse printing in blue as well as the customary green). The middle year of the series generated two misspellings that National Chicle's quality controllers quickly rectified, resulting in scarce variations of Ernie Lombardi ("Earnie") and Hank Greenberg and striking portraits of the issue's Art Deco motif. Greenberg, the recent silver-screen subject of *The Life and Times of Hank Greenberg*, would sit out the 1936 season with a fractured wrist, then miss four years to World War II, yet still retire from baseball in 1947 with totals of 1,276 RBI and 331 home runs. *Estimated Value: $5,000*

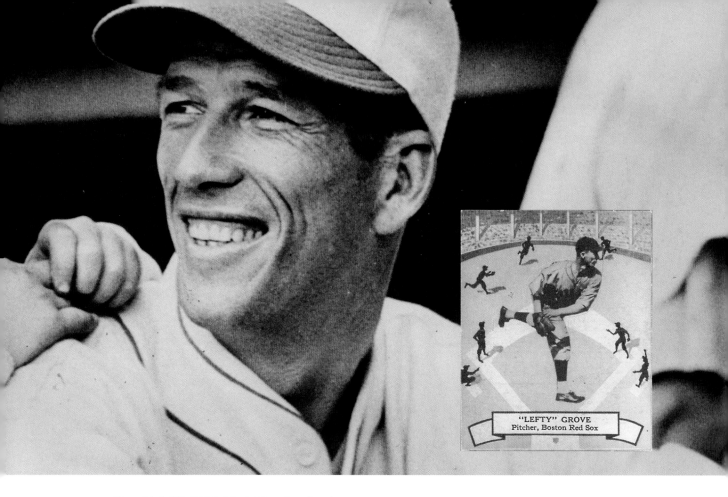

"LEFTY" GROVE
Pitcher, Boston Red Sox

BECAUSE OF ITS SIMILARity to National Chicle's contemporary "Batter-Up" set, O-Pee-Chee's debut offering is often dubbed as "Canadian Batter-Ups." The 40 die-cut cards (numbering 101-140) were distributed exclusively in the provinces and, truth be told, are superior to their predecessors. First and foremost, they're significantly rarer, no doubt because our neighbors to the north cared far more about ice hockey—and, in particular, Montreal Canadiens sensation Howie Morenz—than about baseball. Second, many collectors laud O-Pee-Chee's stylized design, with its action photography, illustrated stadium backdrop, and banner caption. Third, whereas National Chicle's creation has blank backs, Canadian Batter-Ups offer brief biographies—in both English and French! Below the bilingual text is a designation of "Series A," signifying perhaps that a "Series B" of National Leaguers was scheduled to follow the initial all-American-League edition. (In actuality, O-Pee-Chee would not return to baseball-card production until the 1960s, when it began manufacturing Topps sets for release in Canada.) Veteran junior-circuit hurler Lefty Grove was an obvious choice for the elite roster of A.L. ambassadors. Like fellow Hall of Famer Jimmie Foxx, Grove spent his prime years with the Philadelphia Athletics and later migrated to the Boston Red Sox. He never lost more than 13 games in a single season, and he averaged 25 wins per year between 1927 and 1933. A seven-time strikeout leader and *nine*-time ERA king, Grove enjoyed his best campaign in 1931, taking MVP and Triple Crown honors with an astounding 31-4 record, 175 K's, and 2.06 ERA.

Estimated Value: $3,000

1937 V300 O-Pee-Chee #137 — Lefty Grove

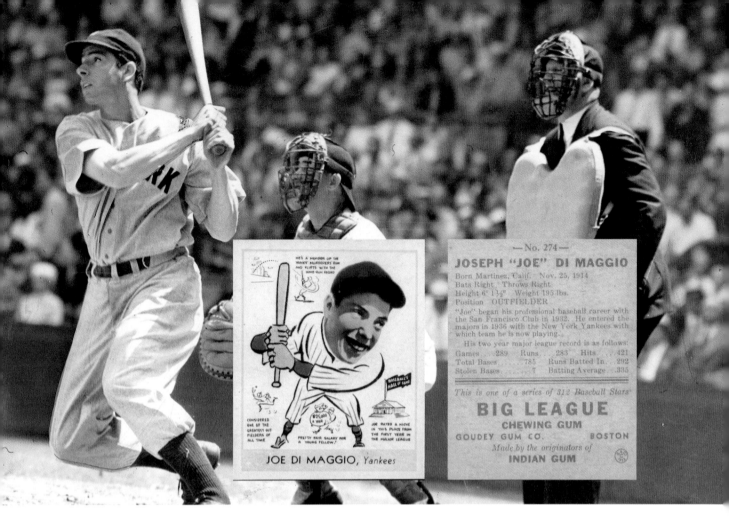

The following is a baseball card depicted in the image:

HE'S A MEMBER OF THE YANKS' MURDERERS ROW AND FLIRTS WITH THE HOME-RUN RECORD

BASEBALL'S HALL OF FAME

CONSIDERED ONE OF THE GREATEST OUT-FIELDERS OF ALL TIME

$25,000 A YEAR

PRETTY FAIR SALARY FOR A YOUNG FELLOW!

JOE RATED A NICHE IN THIS PLACE FROM THE FIRST YEAR IN THE MAJOR LEAGUE

JOE DI MAGGIO, *Yankees*

— No. 274 —

JOSEPH "JOE" DI MAGGIO
Born Martinez, Calif. Nov. 25, 1914
Bats Right Throws Right
Height 6' 1½" Weight 195 lbs.
Position OUTFIELDER

"Joe" began his professional baseball career with the San Francisco Club in 1932. He entered the majors in 1936 with the New York Yankees with which team he is now playing.

His two year major league record is as follows:

Games	289	Runs	283	Hits	421
Total Bases	785	Runs Batted In	292
Stolen Bases	7	Batting Average	.335

This is one of a series of 312 Baseball Stars

BIG LEAGUE
CHEWING GUM
GOUDEY GUM CO.   BOSTON
Made by the originators of
INDIAN GUM

B Y 1938, THE ONCE-STAL-wart Goudey Gum Company was approaching the end of its *belle epoque*. Several sub-par productions and the impending U.S. involvement in World War II had dimin-

most kids, and yet not austere enough to legitimize a childhood pastime such as card collecting in the eyes of adults. Today, of course, connoisseurs recognize 1938 Goudey as a superior vintage that continues to improve with age.

record, a shoo-in Hall of Famer, and "one of the greatest outfielders of all time." Twenty-four ballplayers are each depicted twice in the 48-card release, which is numbered 241 through 288 as a sort of continuation from the check-

1938 R323 Goudey Heads-Up #274 — Joe DiMaggio

ished the firm's profits, resources, and popularity. Nevertheless, Goudey managed to recapture its former glory for the '38 "Heads-Up" set—an ingenious amalgamation of photographic head shots, caricatured bodies, and cartoon backgrounds. The effort met mixed reviews. It was too esoteric for

The set's standard-bearer, Joltin' Joe, grins broadly...and for good reason. His sophomore season had delivered yet another Yankee championship (the second of four titles in DiMaggio's first four years), and Goudey's cartoonists predict that the young Bronx Bomber will prove to be a threat to Ruth's home-run

list of Goudey's '33 set. The only aesthetic difference between the Heads-Up issue's "low-number" and scarcer "high-number" series is that the former features a blank backdrop of white space and the latter showcases its assortment of line-drawing illustrations. *Estimated Value: $9,750*

PLAY BALL BRIDGED THE gap between Goudey's dominance in the early-to-mid 1930s and the birth of Bowman in the late 1940s. The three-set Play Ball series, sponsored by J. Warren out, which would be replicated in Bowman's 1948 offering, presented its subjects in the black-and-white *film noir* elegance of the day. Aspiring to 250 cards, the inaugural edition stopped short at 162 (technically, 161, DiMaggio is "regarded as the greatest outfielder in baseball today." Joltin' Joe's amiable, iconic portrait transports the viewer back to 1939, when *Gone With the Wind* and *The Wizard of Oz* graced the silver screen, and Joseph

1939 R334 Play Ball #26 — Joe DiMaggio

Bowman's Gum, Inc., was something of a test run—or a stepping stone—for the Bowman Gum Company's influential presence in the postwar era. With Goudey and National Chicle effectively closing up shop, Play Ball seized on the opportunity to supplant those earlier bastions of the industry with a new size and style. A caption-less, logo-less lay- since #126 was omitted). By 1939, Babe Ruth and Lou Gehrig had been mustered out of cardboard duty, replaced by the stalwarts of the next generation: a young rookie named Ted Williams and fourth-year standout Joe DiMaggio. According to their biographies on the card-backs, Williams "has a great future according to experts" and Paul DiMaggio Jr. was the toast of the nation, a dashing and heroic symbol of the American melting pot. Here is a card that, in the modern age of exorbitant contracts and steroids scandals, begs that immortal question, "Where have you gone, Joe DiMaggio?" *Estimated Value: $3,250*

"THE NAME IS BERG, Moe Berg." A U.S. undercover agent during World War II, Morris "Moe" Berg has a reputation as the most intelligent and mysterious character in the annals of baseball. He studied linguistics and law at Princeton, Columbia, and the Sorbonne. He played 15 unspectacular seasons as a journeyman utility catcher, averaging 44 games per year and collecting 441 Nicholas Dawidoff's *The Catcher Was a Spy* and Louis Kaufman et al.'s *Moe Berg: Athlete, Scholar, Spy.* The backup backstop got his first taste of espionage in 1934, when he was invited on the major-league "Tour of Japan" under Play Ball card—and was recruited by the Office of Strategic Services (O.S.S.), the predecessor of the CIA. The O.S.S. dispatched him on missions to Norway, Czechoslovakia, and Switzerland, where he consorted with the enemy in order to

1939 R334 Play Ball #103 — Moe Berg

the pretense of his playing abilities (which of course paled in comparison to tour members like Babe Ruth, Lou Gehrig, and Jimmie Foxx). The real reason for his participation was a covert gather intelligence on nuclear development by the Axis powers. After the war, Berg lived a quiet existence—never marrying, never taking a long-term job, but always attending ballgames regu-

```
103     MORRIS BERG
        Catcher    Boston Red Sox
Born: New York City          March 2, 1903
    Bats: Right        Throws: Right
    Height: 6' 1"      Weight: 185 lbs.
Moe Berg is regarded as the most educated
man in baseball, having graduated from Prince-
ton, Columbia, and the Sorbonne, France. Berg
has been a major-league ball player for 18
years, starting in 1923. He is known as one of
the smartest catchers in the game, because of
his ability to handle young pitchers. He started
with Brooklyn as a shortstop, later shifting to
catcher, and has seen action with the Chicago
White Sox, Cleveland Indians, and Washing-
ton Senators, as well as the Red Sox. Moe
spends his off-seasons practicing law, and
globe-trotting, having been around the world
several times. He also speaks fluently eight
different languages.

PLAY BALL — America
This is one of a series of 250 pictures of leading
baseball players. Save to get them all.
GUM, INC., Philadelphia, Pa.   Printed in U. S. A.
```

hits all told. He was a practicing lawyer in the off-season. He spoke eight languages fluently, including German, Russian, Japanese, and Sanskrit. He was misunderstood and shunned by fellow ballplayers for being too cerebral, and for being Jewish. He has been the subject of two biographies, government assignment that he film Tokyo shipyards and military complexes from a hospital rooftop. (Though never confirmed, some have suggested Berg's scouting proved critical during General Doolittle's attacks on the Japanese capital in 1942.) Berg retired from baseball in 1939—the year of this larly—up until his death in 1972. It's a wonder his life story has not yet made it to the silver screen. If it ever does, chances are that Play Ball's chilling, passport-like portrait of the globetrotting catcher-turned-spy will adorn posters and advertisements worldwide.

Estimated Value: $475

119. GROVER CLEVELAND ALEXANDER

Former Major League Pitching Star

Born: St. Paul, Neb.   February 26, 1887
        Batted: Right   Threw: Right
        Height: 6' 1"   Weight: 185 lbs.

(Elected to Baseball Hall of Fame, 1938) Many fans will never forget the time in the World Series of 1926, with the Series tied at three games each between the New York Yankees and the St. Louis Cardinals, when Grover Cleveland Alexander struck out Tony Lazzeri with the bases loaded to win for the Cardinals. Alexander is one of the all-time pitching greats of the National League. He won 373 games, tying Christy Mathewson's record, pitched more shutouts than anybody, 90 from 1911 through 1930, 16 of them in the 1916 season, and three seasons in succession, 1915, '16 and '17, won 30 or more games. He played with the Phillies, Cubs and Cardinals, and only in his last season did he show a percentage under .500.

PLAY BALL

A pictorial news record of America's favorite sport. Save these cards . . . know all about the game and its prominent players. New pictures every year.

© 1940,   GUM, INC., Phila., Pa.   PRINTED IN U. S. A.

"OL' PETE" ALEXANDER

EYOND ITS ROSTER OF contemporary ballplayers, Play Ball's sophomore effort also contained many heroes of yore. One such legend was pitcher Grover Cleveland Alexander, whose birth name had been a tribute to the then commander-in-chief. "Ol' Pete" presided over major-league mounds for 20 stellar seasons (1911-1930), tying Christy Mathewson for third place in all-time victories, with 373. Alexander also holds the single-season record of 16 shutouts, a tally achieved in the middle year of an incredible three-season span, 1915 to 1917, in which he averaged a 31-12 mark and twice captured pitching's statistical Triple Crown. In 1918, Alexander served overseas in World War I. It was a traumatizing experience that would leave him plagued by alcoholism and worsening epilepsy in his postwar seasons. Still, Alexander remained a key contributor to the Chicago Cubs and St. Louis Cardinals throughout the 1920s. The pinnacle of this second phase of his career came in Game 7 of the 1926 World Series, when Alexander struck out Yankee slugger Tony Lazzeri with the bases loaded and then hurled two more scoreless innings to secure a Cardinals championship. After his retirement, the virile veteran continued playing for barnstorming ballclubs, among them the hirsute Hebrew squad known as the House of David. Alexander's life story played out on the big screen in the 1952 film *The Winning Team*, starring Ronald Reagan.

Estimated Value: $450

1940 R335 PLAY BALL #119 — GROVER CLEVELAND ALEXANDER

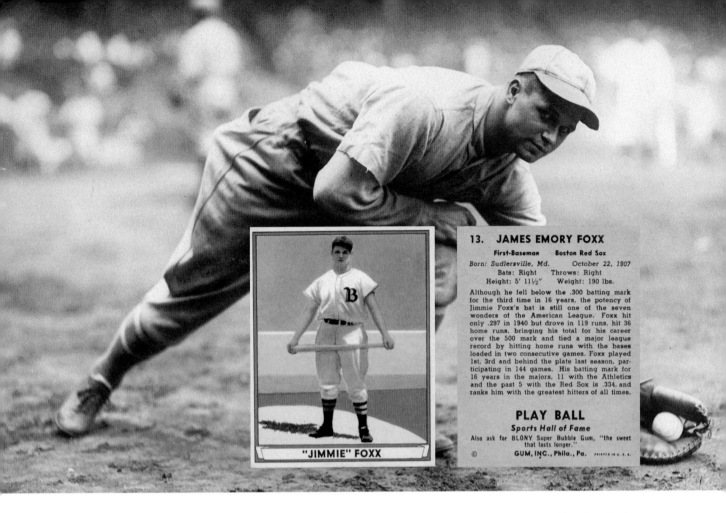

13. **JAMES EMORY FOXX**

First-Baseman   Boston Red Sox

Born: Sudlersville, Md.   *October 22, 1907*
Bats: Right   Throws: Right
Height: 5' 11½"   Weight: 190 lbs.

Although he fell below the .300 batting mark
for the third time in 16 years, the potency of
Jimmie Foxx's bat is still one of the seven
wonders of the American League. Foxx hit
only .297 in 1940 but drove in 119 runs, hit 36
home runs, bringing his total for his career
over the 500 mark and tied a major league
record by hitting home runs with the bases
loaded in two consecutive games. Foxx played
1st, 3rd and behind the plate last season, par-
ticipating in 144 games. His batting mark for
16 years in the majors, 11 with the Athletics
and the past 5 with the Red Sox is .334, and
ranks him with the greatest hitters of all times.

PLAY BALL

Sports Hall of Fame

Also ask for BLONY Super Bubble Gum, "the sweet
that lasts longer."

GUM, INC., Phila., Pa.   PRINTED IN U.S.A.

"JIMMIE" FOXX

HE BEAST. EVEN IN 1941, as a 17-year veteran of the game, Jimmie Foxx still frightened opposing pitchers into submission. Play Ball's biographers described the muscle-bound first baseman in

on record—1932's 58 round-trippers, 169 RBI and .364 average with the Philadelphia Athletics, for example, or 1938's corresponding 50, 175, and .349 with the BoSox. The slugger known in some parts as "Double X"

most major leaguers') last depiction in a full-scale set until after World War II. The 72-card edition has been derided as merely a colorized and abridged version of 1940 Play Ball, however, given the limited wartime resources, it's a

1941 R336 Play Ball #13 — Jimmie Foxx

Babylonian terms, remarking that "the potency of Jimmie Foxx's bat is still one of the seven wonders of the American League." Foxx would plate 100 runners, slam double-digit home runs, and bat .300 for the last time in '41, his final full season with the Boston Red Sox. It was then young Ted Williams' turn to shine in Beantown, and Foxx had already enjoyed some of the finest campaigns

played portions of 1942 and 1944-45 with the Chicago Cubs and Philadelphia Phillies, before taking a position as manager of the Fort Wayne Daisies in the All-American Girls Professional Baseball League—later the basis for Tom Hanks' portrayal of the Rockford Peaches' drunken skipper in *A League of Their Own*. Foxx's inclusion in 1941 Play Ball was his (and, for that matter,

wonder that the issue was produced at all. As a side note, in addition to spotlighting Foxx, Carl Hubbell, Hank Greenberg, and Mel Ott, Play Ball's curtain call also stands as the only set to contain all three DiMaggio brothers. *Estimated Value: $1,800*

CARL HUBBELL
GIANTS—PITCHER

THE GOUDEY GUM Company's last gasp was a modest 33-subject offering headlined by Carl Hubbell and Mel Ott. The blank-backed issue of black-and-white portraits was produced in four different colors—red, blue, yellow, and green—resulting in a motley "master set" of 132 cards that tends to bedevil modern-day collectors. Hubbell's prime years were well behind him, but the lifetime New York Giant was a logical choice for Goudey. Back in 1933, the firm had devoted two cards, #'s 230 and 234, to Hubbell in its debut baseball release, plus had included him as one of only three ballplayers in the 48-card Sport Kings set. In whose noble company did Hubbell revel? None other than Babe Ruth and Ty Cobb. It is only fitting, somehow, that this two-time MVP—known above all else for his 1934 All-Star Game feat of successively striking out Ruth, Lou Gehrig, Jimmie Foxx, Al Simmons, and Joe Cronin—

1941 R324 Goudey #20 — Carl Hubbell

should highlight Goudey's final offering, since the card company had championed him ever since its esteemed beginnings.

Estimated Value: $2,500

*I*N HIS FAMOUS "GREEN LIGHT Letter" of January 15, 1942, President Franklin D. Roosevelt urged Baseball Commissioner Kenesaw Mountain Landis to continue Stan Musial all made their cardboard debuts in the photographic set. A dozen of the entries were randomly short-printed, resulting in an especially sought-after portion of the whole.

1948 Bowman #6 — Yogi Berra

big-league play during World War II, writing, "I honestly feel that it would be best for the country to keep baseball going." Thus, the major leagues rolled on throughout the war years. Baseball cards, however, were a different story. For seven years, the prominent manu-facturers observed a self-imposed "red light" on nationally distributed sets. Bowman finally ended the hiatus in 1948, unveiling its inaugural issue of (fittingly) 48 cards. Yogi Berra, Ralph Kiner, Phil Rizzuto, Warren Spahn, and Bowman expanded to a full-scale 240 cards the following year, and would hold sway in the industry until Topps' emergence several seasons later. As for Berra, the young backstop had already cemented his reputation for quirkiness. He is described on the back of card #6 as "one of baseball's most colorful players." Berra earned a spot on the American League All-Star team that year for the first of 15 consecutive appearances in the mid-summer clas-sic. But alas, despite his stellar on-the-field performance—the 10 champi-onships, three MVP laurels, 350-plus home runs, and commendable .285 lifetime average—Berra will always be remembered most for his "Yogi-isms." Most notable among them, of course, being "It ain't over 'til it's over," "It's déjà vu all over again," and "When you come to a fork in the road...take it."

Estimated Value: $1,200

---

*S*TAN MUSIAL WAS NO freshman when his 1948 Bowman rookie card reached the card-starved public. Rookies do not bat .376 with 39 home runs and 131 played (and had hit over .300) thus far. The unfortunate timing set a precedent for Musial's future card setbacks, name-ly disagreements with the gum compa-nies and, consequently, spotty overall

1948 Bowman #36 — Stan Musial

RBI, missing the N.L. Triple Crown by a single homer. Rookies do not win their third Most Valuable Player award. Musial had never secured cardboard real estate before because of the 7-year wartime production hiatus—precisely how many years "Stan the Man" had representation in 1950s sets. Perhaps a foreboding sense that something was or would be amiss seared Musial with such a stony visage for his inaugural card portrait. Then again, his expression likely speaks more to the intensity and tenacity that typified Musial's 22 seasons of play and that made him a working-class idol to fans in St. Louis and beyond.

Estimated Value: $2,500

8---LEROY (Satchel) PAIGE
Pitcher — Cleveland Indians

Age—40   Bats—right
Ht.—6' 3½"   Throws—right
Wgt.—180 lbs.   Home—Kansas City, Mo.

Most picturesque player in baseball. Has fabulous gate-appeal and high-powered talent to match. Was signed from the Kansas City Monarchs in midsummer of 1948. Finished out the '48 season for the Indians with 6 games won, 1 lost, and 45 strike-outs. Games played: 21, ERA 2.47; pct., .857. Should sizzle into his old stride this year.

ALL-STAR BASEBALL GUM
FREE OF ANY EXTRA COST **BIG PICTURE OF BASEBALL'S GREATEST STARS**

Big 5½" x 7½" portraits, with color background for hanging in your room 'r club. All-time Stars from baseball's Hall of Fame. Give your dealer 10 All-Star Wrappers. He will give you a FREE Portrait.

LEAF GUM CO. Copyright 1949 CHICAGO, ILL.

LEROY PAIGE

WHILE BOWMAN opted for post-war simplicity with small, black-and-white depictions, the Leaf Gum Company produced larger, ostentatiously colorful cards. Leaf's 98-subject set enjoyed an immediate advantage not only in eye-catching graphics but also in star appeal, with a roster boasting Joe DiMaggio, Jackie Robinson, Ted Williams, and even the long-retired Babe Ruth. It was once widely thought that the issue had been released over the course of 1948 and 1949, but experts now agree that it dates solely to 1949. Half of the cards are referred to by hobbyists as the "commons" (including such stars as the Babe!), and the other half itemize as the scarcer "short prints"—of which Satchel Paige is arguably the most coveted exemplar. The second-year pitcher had brought his unorthodox wind-up, cryptic quotations, homespun storytelling, and, most of all, pinpoint pitch control from the Kansas City Monarchs of the Negro Leagues to the Cleveland Indians in 1948. At 42, Paige was the oldest rookie on record. He tallied a 6-1 mark with a 2.47 ERA as the Indians won their second championship in franchise history. Judging from his bemused expression on Leaf's card #8 the following year, Satch was delighted to finally have his chance to shine in the majors and prove, even at his advanced age, what Bob Feller and Joe DiMaggio had asserted all along: Paige was the best pitcher they'd ever seen.

Estimated Value: $42,500

1949 LEAF #8 — SATCHEL PAIGE

No. 226 of a Series of 240

EDWIN "Duke" SNIDER
Outfield—Brooklyn Dodgers
Born: Los Angeles, Calif., September 19, 1926
Bats: Left Throws: Right Ht.: 6:2 Wt.: 175
Duke has tremendous power as a batter. In spring training with the Dodgers he once hit a ball that travelled 500 feet before it stopped rolling. Last season he started with the Dodgers, but wound up with the Montreal Royals where he hit .327, had 17 homers and 177 total bases for his 90 hits. Started in OB in 1944, then went into service.

#202—OFFICIAL BASEBALL RING
Made of durable metal. Adjustable — fits any size finger. Silverplate oxidized finish shows detail of official Baseball Emblem. Baseball of white plastic. Sides show Baseball and Crossed Bats design. Send only 15c and 3 Baseball wrappers to BASEBALL, P.O. BOX 491 NEW YORK 46, N. Y.

(Not valid where contrary to State laws)
Offer expires 12/31/49 ©Bowman Gum, Inc., 1949

EDWIN "Duke" SNIDER

BOWMAN RATCHETED UP the budget, scope, and design for the company's second series. The 48-card total of the previous year blossomed into a 240-subject roster in 1949, and the erstwhile black-and-white layout developed into a bright, though understated motif. The Duke of Flatbush belongs to the coveted high-number contingent. The reverse of card #226 recounts this anecdote of his Herculean, non-steroid-enhanced power: "In spring training with the Dodgers he once hit a ball that traveled 500 feet before it stopped rolling." Snider's first full season saw the Brooklyn outfielder wallop 23 home runs, drive in 92 runs, and bat .292 en route to a Dodgers pennant. Within five years, he would be one of the game's preeminent long-ball hitters and embark on a string of five consecutive 40-homer, 100-RBI campaigns. Snider was also a steely performer in the postseason, collecting 38 hits, 11 round-trippers, and 26 RBI in six World Series. Largely due to Snider and his fellow high numbers, Bowman's 1949 offering is considered its most challenging production to assemble in complete-set form. Young gum-chewers of the day got their first look at the company's colorful new direction with this issue, but to see Bowman's vision evolve further, they would have to heed the words of Snider's fans in Flatbush: "Wait Till Next Year."

1949 Bowman #226 — Duke Snider

Estimated Value: $2,000

No. 100 of a Series of 240
GIL HODGES
Catcher-First Base—Brooklyn Dodgers
Born: Princeton, Ind., April 4, 1924
Bats: Right Throws: Right Ht.: 6:2 Wt.: 195
Almost immediately after Gil was signed by
Dodgers he went into service for three years.
Gil started his career in OB as a third baseman,
and it wasn't until 1946 when he was with
Dodgers' Newport News farm team that he be-
came a catcher. He remained behind plate until
last season when Dodgers switched him to first
base. He played 134 games, hit .250 and batted
in 70 runs.

#202—OFFICIAL BASEBALL RING
Made of durable metal. Adjustable—fits any size
finger. Silverplate oxidized finish shows detail of
official Baseball Emblem. Baseball of white
plastic. Sides show Baseball and
Crossed Bats design. Send only 15c
and 3 Baseball wrappers to:
BASEBALL, P.O. BOX 491
NEW YORK 46, N. Y.
(Not valid where contrary to State laws)
Offer expires 12/31/49 ©Bowman Gum, Inc., 1949

LWAYS A HALL OF Fame hopeful, never a Hall of Famer, Gil Hodges was one of the true-blue "Boys of Summer." His greatest seasons coincided with Brooklyn's glory years of the seven straight seasons with 20 round-trippers and 100 RBI (1949-1955) and won three Gold Glove Awards (1957-1959). He also had a four-home-run game in 1950 and drove in two critical runs in Game 7 of the "Amazin' Mets" to their miraculous '69 championship. Gil Hodges' long, Cooperstown-worthy career actually began with a single game in 1943 that was then followed by three years of World War II service. Resuming his big-

1949 Bowman #100 — Gil Hodges

late 1940s and 1950s, and although he didn't receive the fanfare of Jackie, Campy, Pee Wee, and Duke, Hodges was a dependable workhorse who put up strong offensive numbers and made the big plays at first base. He tabulated Dodgers' 1955 World Series conquest over the Yankees. In 1962, Hodges joined the Big Apple's hapless expansion team, the New York Mets, to whom he would return as manager in 1968— a year before steering the suddenly league aspirations in 1947, Hodges had his first slot in a card set on this burgundy beauty from Bowman's second release.
Estimated Value: $650

Bob Feller (left), dressed in his Navy uniform, and Satchel Paige in 1942.

BOWMAN DABBLED WITH artistic renderings in 1950. It was a year of unrivaled industry clout—the eye of the hurricane, as it were, between foregoing competition by Leaf and the imminent threat of rect the previous year's miscalculations, when an initial overproduction triggered a surplus of excess inventory. Bob Feller surfaces early in the low numbers. He shifts his weight during warm-ups, ready to unwind into a still- to the Indians' rotation in 1946, he picked up where he had left off, pacing the junior circuit in strikeouts and wins once again, while sending a career-high 348 batters down swinging. As late as 1951, the year after this Bowman

1950 BOWMAN #6 — BOB FELLER

Topps. What makes this gorgeous, 252-card release virtually unique among contemporary sets is its topsy-turvy distribution. In contrast to the usual dearth of "high numbers," it is the "low-number series" of cards 1-72 that represents a scarcer population. The back-loaded issue was an effort to cor- potent delivery that recalls his younger days: Fresh out of high school, whiffing 15 batters in his first start, leading the American League in wins and K's from 1939 to 1941. Feller was the first ballplayer of note to sign up for service in World War II—a noble four-year commitment in the end. Returning full-time depiction, Feller was still capable of mustering a 22-8 record on the hill. The fireballer joined Cooperstown's halls in 1962 and, for the past quarter century, has been a constant and beloved figure at baseball-card conventions across the country.
Estimated Value: $950

A limited-release Puerto Rican issue called *Toleteros*, or "Sluggers," contains the only known cardboard depiction of Negro League powerhouse Josh Gibson. Fewer than a dozen no secret. Comparisons to Babe Ruth, tales of Herculean home runs, and assertions that Gibson was the best hitter in history circulated throughout his 17-season career and estimated 962 base-clearing blasts. He and Paige cards should, like theirs, flood this book. However, none of the major producers of the pre- and post-war period—not Goudey, National Chicle, Play Ball, Bowman, Leaf or Topps—featured Gibson in their rosters. The only manu-

1950-51 TOLETEROS — JOSH GIBSON

examples are thought to exist, giving the card an exclusivity more acute than even the T206 Honus Wagner, a.k.a. the "Million Dollar Card." Gibson himself never saw his blue-tinted inclusion were battery mates for the Pittsburgh Crawfords in the 1930s, before Gibson joined the Homestead Grays. Alongside Buck Leonard, Cool Papa Bell, Judy Johnson, Martin Dihigo, facturer to honor this tremendous American talent was a small enterprise in Puerto Rico, where Gibson played winter ball in the off-season. (Interestingly, even the veracity of his Toleteros

JOSHUA GIBSON

Photo Courtesy of PSA

in Toleteros. He had died of a stroke several years earlier, on January 30, 1947—a mere three months shy of seeing Jackie Robinson integrate major-league baseball. Only Satchel Paige claims wider fame than Gibson among the legion of black ballplayers who had their own scheduled seasons, All-Star Games, and World Series from the 1920s through the early 1950s. Yet Paige's acclaim is rooted heavily in his post-Negro League years, when the 42-year-old pitching artist joined the Cleveland Indians. Gibson, too, would have played in the majors, had death not come to him at age 35. The hulking backstop's greatness at the plate was "Smokey" Joe Williams, and Sam Bankhead, Gibson led the Grays to nine consecutive titles between 1937 and 1945. The team split its home games between Pittsburgh's Forbes Field and Washington D.C.'s Griffith Stadium, where first-hand observation led the Washington Senators' Walter Johnson to remark, "*There is a catcher that any big league club would like to buy for $200,000. His name is Gibson. He can do everything. He hits the ball a mile. And he catches so easy, he might as well be in a rocking chair. Throws like a rifle.*" By all accounts, Gibson belongs in the company of the Ruths, Gehrigs, DiMaggios, and Williamses, and his card was in doubt for some time as hobbyists speculated that the subject might be Gibson's son, Josh Gibson Jr., also a Negro League player. However, evidence has recently surfaced that this exact image of Gibson the elder was also used on a Puerto Rican game program dated January 7, 1940, when his son was but 10 years old.) Faced with this paucity of Gibson cards, collectors instead seek out vintage photographs of the legend in Negro League East-West Games and Negro League World Series.

Estimated Value: $50,000

MICKEY MANTLE'S "true" rookie card hit candy-store shelves midway through the '51 season as part of Bowman's high-number series. The tranquil rendering, based on a team-then fostered by the revolution that was Topps' debut offering of 1952—Mantle's first cardboard incarnation has always played second fiddle to its successor. But it's high time to sing '51 Bowman's praises. For starters, the short bio on the reverse conveys the early stages of Mantle's rise to greatness: "Mickey is the Yankee rookie of whom so much is expected in 1951. Everyone was talking about him during spring training in which he batted over

1951 Bowman #253 — Mickey Mantle

issued press photograph, received less fanfare than Mantle's de facto rookie card, the vaunted 1952 Topps #311. By '52, every penny-toting, baseball-loving kid in the land would be clamoring for a talisman of the "Commerce spot-on likeness against a soothing blue-sky canvas represents one of the first images of Mick in a Yankee uniform (incidentally, wearing No. 6 instead of his familiar No. 7). Although the card is not inherently scarce, it does have a .400. Kept on clicking when the regular season got under way." The hard-hitting outfielder would bat .267 with 13 round-trippers and 65 RBI that year, plus capture his first of seven Yankee world championships. Thus the stage

Comet." But back in the thick of 1951, Mick's respectable plate production and inept fielding didn't make front-page news outside the Big Apple; even there, he was matched or overshadowed by Joe DiMaggio's swan-song season, Willie Mays' cross-town might, and Bobby Thomson's "Shot Heard Round the World." For those reasons—reputation for delicateness and difficulty among condition-conscious hobbyists. The pastel colors are susceptible to stains and noticeable print marks, and the thin, white margins seldom exhibit balanced centering. As a result, high-grade examples are not as plentiful as they are for many of Mantle's other standard-issue big-league cards. A was set for the phenomenon of 1952, when young fans regretted trapping their '51 Mantles in bicycle spokes like tattered butterflies, and started craving his much-touted sophomore release with unparalleled anticipation.
Estimated Value: $16,500

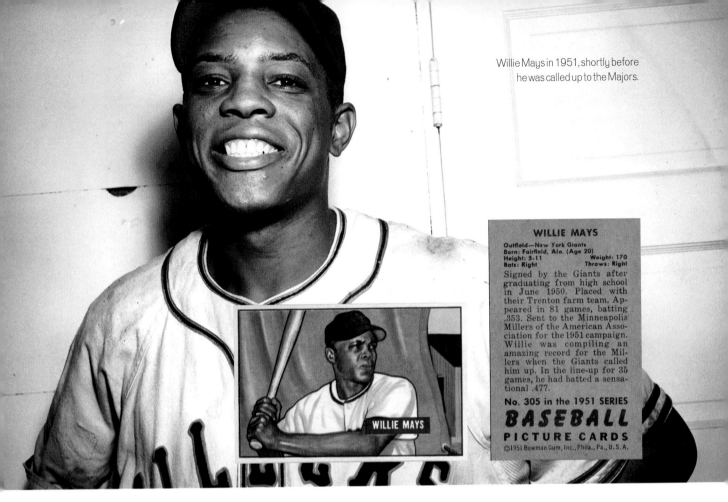

Willie Mays in 1951, shortly before he was called up to the Majors.

WILLIE MAYS

Outfield—New York Giants
Born: Fairfield, Ala. (Age 20)
Height: 5-11   Weight: 170
Bats: Right   Throws: Right

Signed by the Giants after graduating from high school in June 1950. Placed with their Trenton farm team. Appeared in 81 games, batting .353. Sent to the Minneapolis Millers of the American Association for the 1951 campaign. Willie was compiling an amazing record for the Millers when the Giants called him up. In the line-up for 35 games, he had batted a sensational .477.

No. 305 in the 1951 SERIES

BASEBALL
PICTURE CARDS
©1951 Bowman Gum, Inc., Phila., Pa., U.S.A.

WILLIE MAYS

P OISE, GRIT, STRENGTH, power. Straight out of the gate, rookie Willie Mays demonstrated the many traits that would come to define him. Here, his eyes sight the target—a horse-hide orb hurtling within striking distance. Mays swivels his lower body with maximum torque, drives forward his arms, his torso, and clocks the sphere into oblivion. This is the slugger's first card, and his most kinetic. From the steeled visage to the sinewy forearms to the hands fiercely wrapped like tape, Mays pulses with energy, electricity. Anyone who hadn't yet heard of the Giants' versatile centerfielder might have been able to portend his imminent greatness by this image alone. Others had already witnessed a half-season of the Say Hey Kid's diamond talents by the time Bowman included him in its "high-number series." Mays was en route to N.L. Rookie of the Year honors for both his defensive excellence and his offensive production—20 home runs, 22 doubles, 68 RBI, and a .274 batting average. To see the full expression of what he had to offer, fans would have to wait several years. That the young Mays would observe Bobby Thomson's 1951 "Shot Heard Round the World" from the on-deck circle, anticipating his chance at the limelight, was akin to the foreshadowing of fine literature. Mays would be sidelined for almost the entirety of 1952 and 1953 in service to Uncle Sam. Finally, in 1954, he could resume the onslaught he had fomented during his rookie year. Over the next 20 seasons, Mays did just that, appearing in every annual All-Star Game, winning two MVP awards and 12 Gold Gloves, and establishing a legacy as the most complete ballplayer ever to take the field—or to grace a vivid swatch of cardboard.

Estimated Value: $9,000

1951 Bowman #305 — Willie Mays

TOPPS MADE SUCH A splash with its oversized, high-energy release in 1952, it can be easy to forget that the company secured a toehold on the industry in 1951. The main thrust of its first-year be-powerhouse, and the Red Backs/Blue Backs have developed an earnest following among collectors. Any card samples still boasting their original format seen here, a two-part panel, demand a premium in the hobby, as Unfortunately for Roe, he would retire in 1954, one year shy of tasting October glory for himself, with his fellow Dodgers. Both men were in their prime when Topps selected them for the Red Backs—a more star-packed

1951 Topps "Red Back" #5 and #16 Two-Card Panel — Phil Rizzuto/Preacher Roe

operations was a game of sorts, comprising 104 different cards with red- and blue-designed backs. Each portrait hosts an assigned play—ball, strike, single, double, home run, hit by pitcher, most pairs were detached by consumers. The fact that Dodgers hurler Preacher Roe and Yankees shortstop Phil Rizzuto should remain conjoined for posterity is especially surprising, contingent than the scarcer Blue Backs. Roe enjoyed a stunning 22-3 campaign that equated to an .880 winning percentage. Meanwhile, Rizzuto, future mainstay of the Yankees' broad-

etc.—which invariably bears no relation to the respective figure. Indeed, the cards seem to lack any clearly defined rules whatsoever about how the game works. Confusion aside, it was an ambitious freshman effort for the soon-to- what with their teams (and fans) being archrivals. Roe and Rizzuto met in three "Subway Series," each falling in the Yankees' favor as part of seven total championships throughout Rizzuto's war-shortened, 13-season career. casting booth, was riding high after an MVP performance that included 200 hits, 125 runs, a .324 batting average, and a mere 14 errors at short in 155 games. *Holy Cow!*
Estimated Value: $500

SUPPLEMENTING TOPPS' principal offering of Red Backs and Blue Backs in 1951 were three ancillary sets: Team Cards (9), Current All-Stars (11), and Connie Mack's All-Stars (11). The last was a die-till as follows: Babe Ruth, Lou Gehrig, Honus Wagner, Grover Alexander, Mickey Cochrane, Eddie Collins, Jimmy Collins, Christy Mathewson, Walter Johnson, and Tris Speaker. The last of these men, Tristram E Speaker, at-the-plate record for doubles, 793, and fifth-best batting average, .345. For 22 seasons spent mostly in Boston and Cleveland, Speaker was Ty Cobb's greatest rival. In the end, though, Speaker and Cobb's careers inter-

1951 TOPPS CONNIE MACK'S ALL-STARS — TRIS SPEAKER

cut issue saluting legends of yore on the occasion of Manager Mack's retirement after 50 seasons at the helm of the Philadelphia Athletics. Mack poses in his signature vested suit on one of the perforated "stand-up" cards, and his 10 compatriots—depicted head to toe, either batting, pitching, or fielding—dis-extends his body for a daring catch. It is an apt shot of a Hall of Famer who, although best remembered for his offensive production, was as fine an outfielder as ever shepherded stadium pastures. Speaker, or "The Gray Eagle," still holds the lifetime mark for assists, with 450, a suitable complement to his locked. Both were simultaneously implicated in gambling scandals, and both played out their final major-league season, 1928, on the same team— Connie Mack's Athletics.
Estimated Value: $1,500

BEFORE TOTING A Winchester carbine as the title character in TV's western series *The Rifleman* (1958-1963), Chuck Connors wielded another kind of weapon—a baseball bat. The 6-foot-5 dealt to the Chicago Cubs, with whom he started 66 games the next year, contributing 48 hits, a couple of home runs, and a .239 batting average. Returning to the minors in 1952, Connors made a cameo appearance in the regionally Katharine Hepburn, launched Connors' acting career. Soon enough, the former ballplayer found himself known far and wide as Lucas McCain, a frontiersman homesteading in North Fork, New Mexico, with his faithful rifle

1952 MOTHER'S COOKIES #43 — CHUCK CONNORS

first baseman toiled in the Brooklyn Dodgers farm system throughout the 1940s, only to attain, in 1949, one measly at-bat on the major-league level. (The Dodgers' first-base spot was comfortably held by a fellow named Gil Hodges.) In 1950, Connors was finally distributed Mother's Cookies set, a colorful 64-item gallery of Pacific Coast League figures that included old-timers Lefty O'Doul, Stan Hack, and Mel Ott. Then it was goodbye baseball, hello Hollywood. A role in the 1953 film *Pat and Mike*, with Spencer Tracy and and his son Mark. Connors later starred in the films *Geronimo* and *Flipper*, among many others, and in another western-style television serial, *Branded*.

Estimated Value: $1,000

(left to right) Roy Campanella, Don Newcombe, and Jackie Robinson

THE OPTIONS WERE LIM-itless. Campy could be transferred onto one shoulder, Jackie onto the other. Both players could be applied to a notebook, desk, lamp, lunchbox, or baseball bat. For young fans with an eye towards the future, this pair of decals instead could go unused, displayed within its open-window packaging envelope or else socked away for posterity. In 1952, the Meyercord Company of Chicago used hardware stores as the primary retail outlet for its two varieties of Star-Cal decals: individual players (Type 1) and player combos (Type 2). What lad of the 1950s could resist the lure of temporary tattoos trumpeting his favorites heroes of the diamond? Best of all, unlike the inherent mystery in tightly concealed packs of baseball cards, Star-Cals allowed the customer to actually seek out decals of choice among the 68 Type 1's and 32 Type 2's—depending on store availability, of course. In that '52 season, the Boys of Summer played in their third of six "Subway Series" against the Yankees, losing another 7-game heartbreaker that nearly drove Flatbush fans to freefall off the Brooklyn Bridge like so many lemmings. If only those grief-

1952 STAR-CAL DECALS TYPE 2 — ROY CAMPANELLA/JACKIE ROBINSON

stricken mourners could have foreseen the Dodger glory arriving three years hence, when Campy, Jackie, Duke, Pee Wee, and the rest of "Dem Bums" would finally—*finally!*—bring home a championship.
Estimated Value: $500

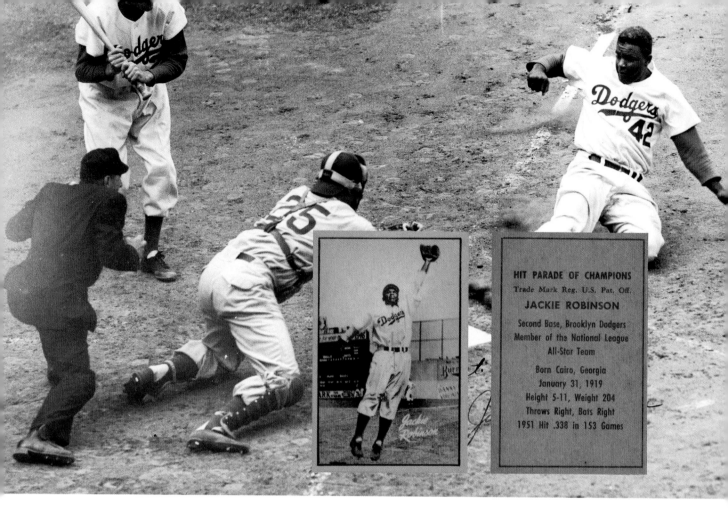

LOST IN THE SHUFFLE OF the Bowman-Topps power struggle in the early 1950s is a two-year release by Berk Ross. The company's 1951 set was a multi-sport edition numbering 40 baseball players out of instead of paired panels. Unlike Bowman and Topps, whose bait-and-switch technique lured young consumers with bubble gum, Berk Ross marketed its wares as "trading cards" to be coveted on their own merits, without

Today, the short-lived "Hit Parade of Champions" series tends to be overlooked by mainstream collectors and adulated by hobbyists with more eclectic taste. Jackie Robinson makes an appearance in the 1952 Berk Ross set.

1952 Berk Ross "Hit Parade of Champions" — Jackie Robinson

72 total entries, all of which were distributed in a two-card-panel format. For its 1952 sequel, Berk Ross focused strictly on baseball, retained the same style of tinted photographs, kept the production run at six dozen, slightly expanded the border dimensions, and disseminated the set as individual cards aid of a sugar incentive. The noble effort was doomed to fail. In a Technicolor age, pastel accents and old-fashioned charm could never compete with Topps' bright, blazing, and modern designs. Berk Ross stepped aside, folded its tent, and became one of the earliest casualties of the Topps revolution.

His leaping full-length pose with the scoreboard in the distance is a magnetic visual tribute to the former Rookie of the Year, National League MVP, and, of course, barrier-breaking civil-rights pioneer.

Estimated Value: $1,300

WAS IT MERE COIN-cidence that Bowman's layout obscured the second half of the word "GRANDSTAND" over Warren Spahn's shoulder? Or was the arrow marked "GRAND" a not-so-sub-

several years. Indeed, Spahn tallied more than 250 of his lifetime wins after age 30! He was also a viable threat at the plate. While most pitchers repre-sent an easy out in the batter's box, Spahn swatted at least one and as

1952 BOWMAN #156 — WARREN SPAHN

liminal message about Spahn's stature on the hill? Either way, the detail was apropos. The winningest southpaw in baseball history, Spahn racked up 363 victories in his 21 seasons—an achieve-ment made even more spectacular by the fact that WWII military service, for which he received the Purple Heart, forestalled the outset of his career by

many as four home runs in every sea-son from 1948 through 1964, setting the current record among all pitchers: 35 career round-trippers. Card #156, in all its grandeur, commemorates the Hall of Famer's last season in Boston before his Braves relocated to Milwaukee. The 252-subject set is one of Bowman's finest creations, though

it has been and always will be up-staged by Topps' landmark issue of the same year.
Estimated Value: $525

CARDS NUMERICALLY first in sets are prone to a dis-proportionate amount of abuse. They were inevitably the top-most card in a sequential stack, mak-ing them acutely vulnerable to sun-

with '52 Topps—the rough adulation natural to awkward, adolescent hands. Pafko's lead-off entry now flaunts itself as a condition rarity of the high-est order and, quite possibly, as the most valuable "common" card in the

1952 TOPPS #1 — ANDY PAFKO

light, incidental contact, soda stains, greasy fingerprints, and, evil of all evils, rubber bands. The most notorious #1 card opens Topps' 1952 release of vibrant, large-sized images that took the card-collecting sphere by storm. Dodger outfielder Andy Pafko bore the brunt of the American baby-boomer youth's smitten infatuation

industry. Lost in the hoopla is Pafko's record as a player. "Handy Andy" logged 17 big-league seasons, all but two (1951-52 in Brooklyn) with the Chicago Cubs and Milwaukee Braves. A reliable ballhawk in the field, he also had three years with 25-plus home runs and four times plated more than 90 runners. Nevertheless, the five-

time All-Star's greatest claim to fame remains his status as the card hobby's number-one #1.
Estimated Value: $15,000

LTHOUGH IT'S NOT HIS rookie card, not his best depiction, not even a rarity, Mantle's 1952 Topps entry reigns as the most coveted production of the great slugger's career—indeed, perhaps of baseball's entire cavalcade of cards. How does a post-war, second-year card of an Oklahoma country boy become the stuff of legend? Timing is everything. The stars aligned for one brief shining year, and Mantle became the torchbearer for the Class of '52.

diamond collectibles. Mantle, too, was the harbinger of a new age. As the card-back presaged, "Switch-hitting Mickey is heralded as Joe DiMaggio's successor." Mick had the good looks, all-American appeal, punishing bat power, big numbers, and, of course, Yankee pin-

1952 TOPPS #311 — MICKEY MANTLE

stripes that made him the obvious leader of the national pastime in general and Topps' inaugural issue in particular. The oversized card was an immediate favorite for trading, flipping, and "spoking," and its larger-than-life stature has

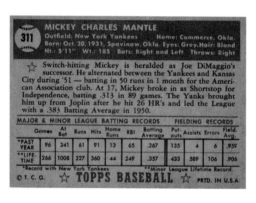

Boasting larger dimensions, dynamic graphics, and a cherished high-number series (that began with #311), an upstart company named Topps staged a cardboard *coup d'état*, usurping the throne from Bowman in much the same way Microsoft laid waste to Apple in the 1990s. Contrary to the phoenix-like Apple, however, Bowman withered and died within a few short years—*topp*led by the vanguard of a new era in

only grown during the past half century. Portrayed in unnaturally bright colors above a facsimile, early-style signature (before Mick starting distinctively looping the first stroke of his "M"), Mantle gazes into the distance—toward his 536 home runs, three MVP laurels, one Triple Crown, 18 World Series home runs, and seven Yankee championships.
Estimated Value: $54,000

Eddie Mathews (second from left) with three Milwaukee Braves teammates.

EDWIN LEE MATHEWS

407

Third Base: Boston Braves   Home: Texarkana, Texas
Born: Oct. 13, 1931, Texarkana, Texas   Eyes: Blue
Ht.: 6'1"   Wt.: 185   Hair: Brown   Bats: Left   Throws: Right

☆ Milwaukee was Ed's first and last minor league team prior to his being brought up by the Braves in April of '52. He broke in with the Brewers in '49 but played most of his ball with Thomasville that year where he batted .363 in 63 games. He started the '50 season with Milwaukee and was sent down to Atlanta. He started the '51 season with Atlanta and returned to Milwaukee. Ed hit 32 Homers in 1950.

	MINOR LEAGUE BATTING RECORD							FIELDING RECORD			
	Games	At Bat	Runs	Hits	Home Runs	RBI	Batting Average	Put-outs	Assists	Errors	Field. Avg.
PAST YEAR	49	137	25	40	7	44	.292	31	62	7	.930
LIFE-TIME	258	929	190	285	56	196	.307	261	406	52	.928

© T. C. G.   ☆ **TOPPS BASEBALL** ☆   PRTD. IN U.S.A.

ED MATHEWS

Edwin Lee Mathews

BOSTON BRAVES ROOKIE Eddie Mathews enjoys the unique privilege of closing out the most ground-breaking set in baseball history. Every cherished facet of '52 Topps rings true here—the grand young sluggers would come to dominate the home-run leader board throughout the 1950s and 1960s, and they would cross the 500-HR plateau together in 1967—Mantle on May 14 and Mathews exactly two months later ing start with 25 round-trippers. In '53, he unloaded for 47 base-clearing blasts—a longstanding record for National League third basemen and Mathews' first in a string of nine straight 30-plus-homer seasons. The only play-

1952 TOPPS #407 — EDDIE MATHEWS

size, compelling portrait, sparkling hues, and marquee-like caption box promoting name, signature, and team emblem. It seems to have been written in the stars that Mickey Mantle and Mathews should bookend the issue's revered high-number series. Both on July 14. The pair also met twice in the World Series (1957-1958), their first encounter falling in Mathews' favor and the second adding yet another championship ring to Mantle's collection. As a big-league freshman in 1952, Mathews got his career off to a rollick- er to suit up for the Braves in Boston, Milwaukee, and Atlanta, Mathews retired in 1968 after a partial season with that year's world champion Detroit Tigers. His 512 career homers currently tie him for 17th on the all-time list. *Estimated Value: $20,000*

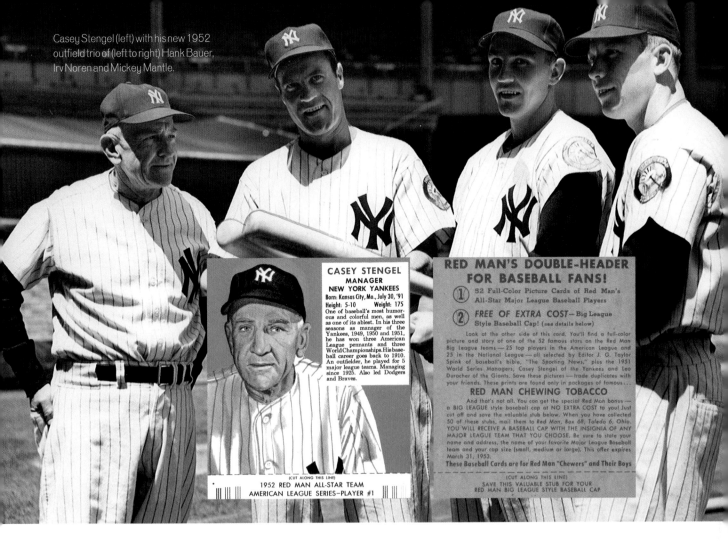

Casey Stengel (left) with his new 1952 outfield trio of (left to right) Hank Bauer, Irv Noren and Mickey Mantle.

CASEY STENGEL
MANAGER
NEW YORK YANKEES
Born: Kansas City, Mo., July 30, '91
Height: 5-10   Weight: 175
One of baseball's most humorous and colorful men, as well as one of its ablest. In his three seasons as manager of the Yankees, 1949, 1950 and 1951, he has won three American League pennants and three World Championships. His baseball career goes back to 1910. An outfielder, he played for 5 major league teams. Managing since 1925. Also led Dodgers and Braves.

(CUT ALONG THIS LINE)
1952 RED MAN ALL-STAR TEAM
AMERICAN LEAGUE SERIES—PLAYER #1

RED MAN'S DOUBLE-HEADER FOR BASEBALL FANS!
① 52 Full-Color Picture Cards of Red Man's All-Star Major League Baseball Players
② FREE OF EXTRA COST— Big League Style Baseball Cap! (see details below)

Look at the other side of this card. You'll find a full-color picture and story of one of the 52 famous stars on the Red Man Big League teams — 25 top players in the American League and 25 in the National League — all selected by Editor J. G. Taylor Spink of baseball's bible, "The Sporting News", plus the 1951 World Series Managers; Casey Stengel of the Yankees and Leo Durocher of the Giants. Save these pictures — trade duplicates with your friends. These prints are found only in packages of famous...

RED MAN CHEWING TOBACCO

And that's not all. You can get the special Red Man bonus — a BIG LEAGUE style baseball cap at NO EXTRA COST to you! Just cut off and save the valuable stub below. When you have collected 50 of these stubs, mail them to Red Man, Box 68, Toledo 6, Ohio. YOU WILL RECEIVE A BASEBALL CAP WITH THE INSIGNIA OF ANY MAJOR LEAGUE TEAM THAT YOU CHOOSE. Be sure to state your name and address, the name of your favorite Major League Baseball team and your cap size (small, medium or large). This offer expires March 31, 1953.

These Baseball Cards are for Red Man "Chewers" and Their Boys

(CUT ALONG THIS LINE)
SAVE THIS VALUABLE STUB FOR YOUR
RED MAN BIG LEAGUE STYLE BASEBALL CAP

*T*HE SEGMENT ON which the entire hobby is founded, tobacco cards, enjoyed a brief renaissance and then came to its end with a four-year issue by Red Man Tobacco in the early to middle carried a perforated tab along the bottom that, at least in the eyes of modern hobbyists, was best left intact. Instead, these tabs were usually removed, and sometimes in a careless way that wrought more damage on the already-editions. Stengel, who then bore the lines of age from 14 seasons as a player and more than a dozen as a skipper, would continue managerially for another decade after Red Man ceased producing cards. Five more pennants and

1952 RED MAN #1 — CASEY STENGEL

1950s. Like their ancestors of the 1880s to 1910s, Red Man cards suffered the fate of a perilous packaging environment. The large, square inserts were encased in a thin plastic sleeve on the outside of pouches of tobacco, making creases unavoidable even before the cards reached consumers. Furthermore, each illustrated depiction pawed collectibles. Ballplayers Ted Williams, Duke Snider, Stan Musial, Willie Mays, and Yogi Berra highlighted Red Man's 204-card series, but *numero uno* was a manager, one Casey Stengel. In the midst of five straight championships at the Yankees' helm, the future Hall of Famer lent his scholarly countenance to the 1952 and 1953 two championships with the Yankees, plus four dismal seasons managing the lowly New York Mets, awaited the "Old Professor," and he would be enshrined with a plaque at Cooperstown just one year after his retirement.
Estimated Value: $550

STAN MUSIAL ☆

NO. 32

Outfield — St. Louis Cardinals
Born: Donora, Pa., November 21, 1920
Height: 6 feet; Weight: 175; Bats: Left; Throws: Left

The mere mention of "Stan, the Man" suffices for most baseball fans, because he's the greatest. For the third straight year, the sixth time in his career, Stan was the National League batting champion with an average of .336. He tied for leadership in runs scored with 105, making nine consecutive seasons he has scored 100 or more runs. He had the most base hits, 194.

| | MAJOR LEAGUE BATTING RECORD | | | | | | FIELDING RECORD | | | |
	Games Played	Times at Bat	Runs Scored	No. of Hits	Home Runs	Runs Bat. In	Bat. Ave.	Put Outs	No. of Assists	No. of Errors	Field. Ave.
Post Year	154	578	105	194	21	91	.336	502	18	5	.991
Life time	1524	5844	1149	2023	227	1014	.352	6340	308	73	.989
This Year											

© B.G.H.L.I. **BASEBALL COLLECTOR SERIES** Printed in U.S.A.

E WASN'T THE strongest, the fastest, or the flashiest. He didn't have Duke Snider's power, Willie Mays' speed, or Mickey Mantle's panache. But Stan was "The Man." He was a blue-collar hero that punched in each day, put in a determined, reliable effort, and clocked out at day's end. If double-duty was required, Musial worked twice as hard. In a 1954 twin-bill against the New York Giants, he blasted five home runs—the first player ever to do so. Year after year, the three-time MVP winner was consistency personified, batting well over .300, knocking in 100 runs, swatting a few dozen home runs, and collecting 30 to 40 doubles. After 22 seasons, he retired second only to Ty Cobb in lifetime hits with 3,640 (since surpassed by Hank Aaron and Pete Rose). In St. Louis, Stan Musial was the best thing since Charles Lindbergh. The humility, enthusiasm, and wholesomeness that so endeared him to Cardinals fans are on full display in this card #32 from the beloved 1953 Bowman Color set. Here is a man—The Man—that loved his lot in life. Although Musial has not sustained the star power of his major-market colleagues—the DiMaggios, Williamses, and Mantles—he certainly held his own back in the day. As the cardback succinctly states, "The mere mention of 'Stan, the Man' suffices for most baseball fans because he's the greatest."

Estimated Value: $1,450

1953 BOWMAN COLOR #32 — STAN MUSIAL

☆ HAROLD "Peewee" REESE ☆

NO. 33

Shortstop — Brooklyn Dodgers
Born: Ekron, Ky., July 23, 1919
Height: 5-9½; Weight: 178; Bats: Right; Throws: Right

The Dodgers' team Captain, Pee Wee is one of the most popular and respected players in baseball. He is also one of the best. He was selected by the New York Baseball Writers as the Player of the Year for 1952. He led the League in stolen bases with 30. In the fielding department his percentage was .969, just three points away from the best in the league. He's been with Brooklyn since 1940.

| | MAJOR LEAGUE BATTING RECORD | | | | | | | FIELDING RECORD | | | |
	Games Played	Times at Bat	Runs Scored	No. of Hits	Home Runs	Runs Bat. In	Bat. Ave.	Put Outs	No. of Assists	No. of Errors	Field. Ave.
Past Year	149	559	94	152	6	58	.272	282	376	21	.969
Life time	1431	5378	894	1447	79	602	.270	2940	4216	282	.962
This Year											

© B.G.H.L.I. **BASEBALL COLLECTOR SERIES** Printed in U.S.A.

HIGH-FLYING PEE WEE Reese gives new meaning to being a "Dodger." Instead of darting aside trolley cars, the derivation of Brooklyn's team moniker, Reese leaps straight up to avoid a sliding runner. He floats several feet above second base, almost as if kneeling on an invisible magic carpet, and he cocks his arm for a laser throw to first. The spring-training action shot is the prototypical card from an atypical set. Bowman's antepenultimate offering remains a favorite among collectors, not necessarily because of value or scarcity but for its supreme visuals. The white-bordered, Technicolor-bright images stand on their own. Captions, player names, elaborate designs, team logos, company emblems, copyright information—all of these details that come to dominate other sets are absent in 1953 Bowman Color. Reese's card #33 represents the zenith of the sleek, entrancing style. Devoid of any distractions, there is only the Dodger captain, his dead-to-rights victim, the hazy sky, the expansive field. Any youngster who ripped open a pack and feasted eyes on this sight would have immediately identified the subject, without any legend stating the obvious: "Harold 'Pee Wee' Reese." Seeing Reese "turn two" in mid-air paints an entire, time-honored sequence of events: Second baseman Jackie Robinson scoops up a blazing

1953 BOWMAN COLOR #33 — PEE WEE REESE

grounder and slings it to Reese, who in one fluid motion deftly grazes the bag, dodges the barreling baserunner, and rifles the ball with heat and precision to first baseman Gil Hodges for the 4-6-3 double play...and the Flatbush faithful go wild!

Estimated Value: $1,500

The husky backstop is recognized as one of the great fielding catchers of all time. He is also a powerful hitter as his Home Run record will attest. "Campy" was up among the League's batting leaders during the 1st part of the '52 campaign but injuries slowed him up. He finished 2nd on the Dodgers in HR's and RBI's in '52. In '51 he hit .325, slammed 33 HR's and was the Most Valuable Player in the National League. Roy was on every All-Star team since '49.

H AS ANY PLAYER EVER looked happier on a baseball card? Burly backstop Roy Campanella had good reason to smile in '53. His 41 home runs and 142 RBI both set records among catchers, and the former Rookie of the Year now added a second MVP to his trophy case. It was roughly the halfway point in Campy's 10-season career, abruptly cut short in 1958 by the vehicular catastrophe that henceforth restricted him to a wheelchair. Statistically inclined baseball fans often lament how the lost wartime seasons of Ted Williams and Hank Greenberg adversely affected their career numbers. Campanella suffered a similar fate, for his 242 round-trippers and 856 RBI neglect to measure seven seasons spent in the Negro Leagues plus the would-be stats of his post-accident years. As to Topps' 1953 edition—which was re-released to a new generation of collectors in 1991 as "1953 Topps Archives"—hobbyists generally view it as a mixed blessing. The artwork is exquisite, but the condition unreliable. Off-centering afflicts the white margins, and the full-bleed caption area (red for the American League, black for the National League) betrays even the subtlest signs of edge or corner wear. But who can blame the rambunctious youngsters of the 1950s for their tactile enthusiasm? Cards were meant for flipping and trading, rubber-banding and poring over, not socking away in a safety deposit box. *Baseball cards, worth thousands and thousands of dollars someday?! Not a chance. Impossible.*
Estimated Value: $600

1953 TOPPS #27 — ROY CAMPANELLA

AT 46, THE TIMELESS, enigmatic "Satch" was in the midst of his last major-league campaign. The St. Louis Browns, Paige's hapless team of three seasons, also were in a transitional stage—metamorphosing into the Baltimore Orioles by 1954. Paige's statistics for the year—3 wins, 9 losses, 11 saves, and a 3.53 ERA—are less than stellar, unless seen in the proper context, i.e., the Browns' pitiable last-place record of 54-100. Nevertheless, 1953 was not without its glory for the hard-traveled veteran of the majors, Negro Leagues, and innumerable barnstorming tours. On July 14 at Cincinnati's Crosley Field, Paige became the first black American Leaguer to pitch in an All-Star Game. Yankee Manager Casey Stengel had named him to the junior-circuit squad in 1952, on the strength of what would be arguably Paige's best showing: a 12-10 mark with 2 shutouts, 10 saves, and a 3.07 ERA. That midsummer classic was rained out in the fifth inning, however, and the Browns' right-hander never entered the game. Stengel promised him another chance the next year and, despite Paige's lack-luster numbers in '53, the "Old Professor" kept his word. Satch was elected to his second All-Star contest, and Stengel called him in for the eighth inning. Paige retired at season's end, although on a lark he did take the mound again for the Kansas City Athletics in 1965. The 59-year-old icon hurled three scoreless innings. His artistic portrait on #220 of Topps' second major offering delivers the qualities for which baseball fans still treasure Satchel Paige's memory—wit, wisdom, strength, poise, and dignity. *Estimated Value: $2,200*

1953 Topps #220 — Satchel Paige

"**T**ED IS ONE OF THE GREATEST!" proclaims the exuberant typescript on the reverse. *"He returned to the Red Sox late in 1953 after serving in Korea as a Marine Captain and air pilot. Had a close shave in Korea when his plane was hit by enemy aircraft,* its set. Bowman, meanwhile, was forced to pull from its press the Boston hero's sunny disposition for lack of proper authorization to use his image. The coup portended events yet to unfold: Bowman's collapse and Topps' ascendence. In Williams' stead surfaced a new #66, fellow

1954 BOWMAN #66 —
TED WILLIAMS

but he made it back to the landing strip on a wing and a prayer.' Ted got into 37 games in 1953 and hit .407. He had 13 home runs and drove in 34 runs, proving he hadn't lost the touch." For Williams, touch was only part of the formula for

Beantowner Jimmy Piersall, who himself already graced card #210. The Williams-for-Piersall exchange resulted in a total of 225 entries, rather than the predicted 224, and established one of the scarcest standard-issue

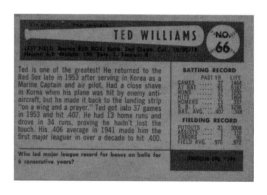

success. Legend has it that his eye sight was so keen he could actually see the rotation of pitched baseballs. And then there was the sheer quickness of his bat. Returning to the full-time lineup in 1954, the Boston icon exceeded all expectations by batting .345 with 89 RBI and 29 home runs. Unfortunately for Bowman, the company's excitement about featuring "Teddy Ballgame" for the first time since 1951 was short-lived. Upstart competitor and imminent usurper Topps claimed Williams as its own in '54, bookending him as the first and last card in

cards in the entire Bowman or Topps catalogs. Hobbyists consider Williams' wholesome, feel-good portrait to be the centerpiece of Bowman's second-to-last release. Interestingly, although the gum-maker lost to Topps in the "Williams War," Bowman did scoop its rival—as it had in 1951 as well—on a younger ballplayer by the name of Mickey Mantle, who is absent from 1954 Topps yet holds forth as #65 in 1954 Bowman.

Estimated Value: $6,250

HENRY AARON
outfield MILWAUKEE BRAVES

HENRY LOUIS AARON   outfield MILWAUKEE BRAVES

ONE WOULD THINK THAT baseball's Home Run King would always be depicted with a bat in hand. But back in '54, Hammerin' Hank was known only as Henry Aaron, and Topps chose not to highlight his prowess at the plate, but rather the lanky rookie's deft glovework in the field. Even the card's reverse notes that Aaron paced the Sally League the year before in batting average, RBI, hits, runs, total bases and doubles—with no mention of round-trip-

pers! Indeed, the young Milwaukee Brave was a talked-about prospect for every reason except the one that would make him a diamond immortal. Aaron circled the bases a mere 13 times his first year in the majors (in no small part due to a broken ankle in early September), yet never fell below 20 homers again for the next 20 seasons— a streak that even in our current era of Herculean longballers has yet to be repeated. Some attribute Hank's unmatched power to the forceful snap

of his wrists, strengthened while carrying huge blocks of ice door-to-door as a teenager, delivering the frozen slabs to owners of non-electric refrigerators for a few dollars a day. Here, Aaron is not so far removed from his formative Ice Age, and his face shows the exuberance and vigor of a 20-year-old whose future is as bright as the jack-o'-lantern orange background that surrounds him.
Estimated Value: $3,000

1954 TOPPS #128 — HANK AARON

THE COPYWRITERS AT Topps recognized Ernie Banks' potential right from the start, noting on the reverse of his rookie card, "*After gaining recognition as the top* *bases and looks like a real hot prospect* *for a regular Bruin infield berth this sea-* *son.*" Banks would be a fixture in the "Friendly Confines" of Wrigley Field for the next 19 years. Cementing himself in Games. His first-year portrait showcases the winning smile and positivity that so endeared "Mr. Cub" to Chicago's Northsiders. Interestingly, Topps' 1954 set was the first baseball issue to

1954 TOPPS #94 — ERNIE BANKS

ranking player in the Negro National *League, Ernie came to the Cubs* *from the Kansas City Monarchs in* *September 1953. Seeing only limited* *service with Chicago last year, the for-* *mer Army Artilleryman hit for 22 total* the record books as baseball's hardest-hitting shortstop, he collected 512 career home runs and five times walloped more than 40 homers in a single season. Along the way, Banks won two MVP awards and played in 11 All-Star deliver two player pictures on each single-subject card. Banks certainly approved of his dual appearances. As the enthusiastic infielder liked to say on game day, "Let's play two!"
Estimated Value: $2,200

THE COMBINATION OF baseball cards and potato chips required special precautions. In an attempt to ward off the grease stains of incidental contact inside the bag, Dan-Dee covered its 29 insert cards with an extra-thick wax coating. What the manufacturer could not hope to protect against, however, was the oily hands of young buyers. There was no time lapse between admiring a new card and gobbling salty, glistening chips; the lure of instant grati- fication rendered both actions simultaneous. Consequently, even those Dan-Dees that managed to survive their packaging in an unsullied state tended to wind up fingerprint-ridden by Day One outside their sealed confines. The condition-sensitive release is dominated by Cleveland Indians and Pittsburgh Pirates, but Mickey Mantle's affable portrait represents the key card in the set. On the reverse, a brief bio of the fourth-year star reports, "*Potentially the greatest player in baseball today, his career has been threatened by a knee injury received in the 1952 World Series. Underwent an operation this spring to eliminate the trouble. A switch hitter, he's a distinct homer threat from either side. Is fastest man in American League.*" The 1954 season marked several firsts for Mantle. He eclipsed 25 home runs, plated more than 100 runners, and finally went home at season's end *without* a Yankees championship. *Estimated Value: $6,500*

1954 DAN-DEE POTATO CHIPS — MICKEY MANTLE

IN 1954, THE "SAY HEY KID" returned to baseball after two years of military service. New York Giants fans were overjoyed to have their rising star back in uniform, and Mays was chomping at the bit to show during Game 1, and claiming his first of two MVP laurels. That year, Mays also made his cardboard comeback. He appeared in the mainstream sets of Topps and Bowman, as well as in the smaller issues for Red Man Tobacco

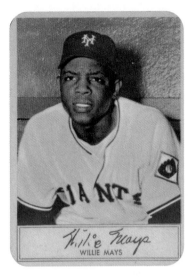

1954 Stahl-Meyer Franks — Willie Mays

that his sensational rookie season had been no fluke. He made up for lost time by putting up huge numbers (41 home runs, 110 RBI, 13 triples, 33 doubles, and a .345 batting average), lifting his New York Giants to a 4-game World Series sweep of the Cleveland Indians, making "The Catch" in deep centerfield and Stahl-Meyer Franks. Stahl-Meyer distributed its second of three annual editions featuring select players from the trio of New York teams—the Giants, Yankees, and Dodgers. Mays leans forward on the dugout bench in his yellow-bordered, round-cornered depiction, anxiously waiting in the wings for his long-forestalled second chance at the limelight.

Estimated Value: $2,500

UNLIKE OTHER REgional, food-promotion issues that cropped up around the same time—Dan-Dee Potato Chips, Wilson Franks, Stahl-Meyer Franks—Red Hearts were Dog Food," was meant for Rover. Thirty-three big leaguers imparted their likenesses to the brightly colored one-year release, including Mickey Mantle, Stan Musial, Nellie Fox, Ralph Kiner, Duke Snider, Ted Kluszewski, and the Phillies'

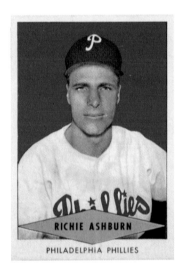

1954 Red Heart Dog Food — Richie Ashburn

redeemable by mail. They weren't packaged with greasy, meaty, or crumby products, and so have survived in greater numbers and superior condition than their peers. Actually, there is another distinction: Dan-Dee Chips et al. were intended for human consumption; Red Heart, a.k.a. "The Big League reliable lead-off hitter Richie Ashburn. Ashburn's popularity in the City of Brotherly Love stems as much from his three decades in the broadcast booth as from his dozen seasons patrolling the outfield of Shibe Park and Connie Mack Stadium. Nonetheless, it was his .308 lifetime average, 2,574 safeties, and .983 fielding percentage that earned "Whitey" a 1995 induction to Cooperstown.

Estimated Value: $325

IF THIS WERE A COMIC-STRIP frame, there might be a "thought bubble" leading from Ted's noggin to the 12-pack of hot dogs floating in the ether. The concept would be that even while swinging for the fences, the dozen dogs in their shiny protective wrap served as the identifying logo on every one of the 20 cards sold with Wilson Franks in 1954. Among the bevy of the era's food-brand issues— Johnston Cookies, Dan-Dee Potato mishaps—all of which have contributed to a scant number of complete sets, let alone those in high grade. Current and should-be Hall of Famers Bob Feller, Roy Campanella, Enos Slaughter, Red Schoendienst, Gil Hodges, and

1954 WILSON FRANKS — TED WILLIAMS

Splendid Splinter simply cannot get Wilson Franks off his mind. They tantalize him, driving Williams to hit a homer sooner, win the game sooner, and indulge in America's favorite processed meat sooner. In all seriousness, though, Chips, Briggs Meat, and the like—this one-year edition is perhaps the cream of the crop. A majority of extant cards endured freezer-case temperatures, shopping-cart piles, check-out carelessness, and, finally, wrap-removal Nellie Fox share the Wilson Franks roster with Williams, whose fluid follow-through is as elegant a picture as ever graced card stock—floating hot dogs notwithstanding.

Estimated Value: $32,500

THIS 66-CARD ILLUS-trated set put a modern spin on the classic design advanced back in 1911 by Mecca Double Folders. Two players occupy opposite sides of stance would be replaced by his Brooklyn Dodgers teammate Don Hoak's fielding pose. At the time, these two infielders were headed in opposite directions. Hoak was a young prospect Brooklyn baseball, when "Dem Bums" finally conquered their cross-town rival New York Yankees. Five years later, Hoak would again taste sweet victory over the Yankees, this time with the

1955 Topps Doubleheaders #25–26 – Jackie Robinson/Don Hoak

each card and, once a horizontal fold has created the necessary hinge, share a single pair of lower legs. In this instance, Jackie Robinson's batting in just his second major-league season, Jackson an aging veteran in his second-to-last campaign. Both earned championship rings in that most storied year of underdog Pittsburgh Pirates in a seven-game World Series capped off by Bill Mazeroski's heroic walk-off home run. *Estimated Value: $1,500*

ROBERTO WALKER CLEMENTE
outfield Pittsburgh Pirates

164

Height: 5'11"
Weight: 175
Bats: Right
Throws: Right
Home: Carolina, P. R.
Born: Aug. 18, 1934

Roberto was the Pirates' 1st choice at the 1954 Winter Draft. Originally signed by the Dodgers to a bonus contract, he showed his powerful throwing arm and extra base hitting ability at Montreal last year. During the Winter, Roberto played in the Puerto Rican League and placed 2nd in hitting. His 73 hits at Santurce gave him a glittering .365 Batting Average.

DAFFY-NITIONS

WHAT IS A "HOOK" IN BASEBALL?

ANS: A curve ball.

MINOR LEAGUE BATTING RECORD									FIELDING			
	Games	At Bat	Runs	Hits	2b	3b	H.R.	R.B.I.	B.Avg.	P.O.	Assists	Errors	F.Avg.
Year	87	148	27	38	5	3	2	12	.257	81	1	1	.988
Life	87	148	27	38	5	3	2	12	.257	81	1	1	.988

ROBERTO CLEMENTE outfield PITTSBURGH PIRATES

*T*OPPS UNVEILED A NEW look in '55. The company took its previous year's portrait-and-action-pose motif and turned it on its side—literally. Along with the zest of horizontality came the comforts of conjured in 1955 and henceforth at the mere mention of the outfielder's name. In the "Steel City," kids would commit the reverse to memory, too: *"Roberto was the Pirates' 1st choice at the 1954 Winter Draft. Originally signed by the* career, his celebrity rose to saintly stature in the wake of the Puerto Rican hero's death on New Year's Eve in 1972. Ever the humanitarian, Roberto was on his way to deliver aid supplies in earthquake-ravaged Nicaragua when

1955 TOPPS #164 — ROBERTO CLEMENTE

Topps' standard fare: a kaleidoscope of colors, a stellar roster, a rarefied "high-number series," and the impassioned depictions that young fans would emblazon in their minds as the definitive visual identities of their favorite players. And so it was when pack-buyers first glimpsed Pirates prospect Roberto Clemente. This rookie image would be *Dodgers to a bonus contract, he showed his powerful throwing arm and extra base hitting ability at Montreal last year. During the Winter, Roberto played in the Puerto Rican League and placed 2nd in hitting. His 73 hits at Santurce gave him a glittering .365 Batting Average."* As popular as Clemente was during his 3,000-hit, 12-Gold-Glove his plane crashed in the ocean. He was 38. Knowing this looming fate transforms the card from an innocent portrayal to a glorious homage, one honoring a great ballplayer and an even greater man.

Estimated Value: $4,600

1955 Topps #123 — Sandy Koufax

GROWING UP, BASKET-ball was Sandy Koufax's first love; baseball was an afterthought. The Brooklyn sandlots were a place to spend time with friends, not to hone a curve. The high-school diamond meant an extracurricular activity for the hardcourt off-season, not a stepping stone to any future in baseball—let alone a Hall of Fame pitching career. It was a hoops scholarship that brought Koufax to the University of Cincinnati, but once again Sandy was drawn to the pitcher's mound as well (in part because UC's basketball coach Ed Jucker doubled as the school's baseball skipper). When major-league scouts showed up to see Koufax's uncommon talents, the southpaw finally accepted his fate. Baseball had been chasing him since childhood; it was time to trade his sneakers for cleats, once and for all. The next year, Koufax greeted the country on card #123 and, on the reverse, Topps had this to say about him:

"The Dodgers took a big step in bolstering their mound corps when they signed Sandy for a large bonus last season. The former University of Cincinnati hurler compiled a brilliant Strikeout record at college. In 30 innings at Cincinnati, he struck out 58 men and posted 34 SO's in 2 consecutive games."

What a year to arrive in—or, in Koufax's case, return to—Brooklyn. Sandy collected the first of his three championship rings in '55. He wouldn't hit his stride until 1961, after the team had moved west to Los Angeles. There, Koufax strung together arguably the most dominating five-year stretch in baseball history...and then retired at the pinnacle of his career. He averaged 22 wins, 7 losses, and 1.98 earned runs, while also compiling two championships, four no-hitters, one perfect game, an MVP selection, and three Cy Young Awards. Idolized by many, he was especially revered by Jewish fans, who hadn't seen a Jewish ballplayer the likes of Koufax since Detroit slugger Hank Greenberg. Koufax was king of the hill in the early to middle sixties. Basketball's loss had become baseball's immeasurable gain.

Estimated Value: $1,850

Major-league umpires in their
signature garb circa 1920s.

Cal Hubbard
UMPIRE SUPERVISOR, A. L.

All-time great tackle with Green Bay Packers
1929, 1930, 1931, 1932, 1933 and 1935 and
New York Giants 1927, 1928 and 1936.
Residence, Milan, Missouri. Born October
31, 1900, at Keyteville, Missouri. Hobby is
bird hunting. Scotch-Irish descent. Graduate
of Geneva College in 1927. Began umpiring
with Piedmont League in 1928 and American
League umpire since 1936. He was named
Umpire Supervisor in January of 1954 succeeding Tommy Connolly. Umpire in four
World Series and three All-Star games.

©B.G.H.L.I.   PRINTED IN U.S.A.

QUESTIONS
1. In what year did
the New York
Giants win 26
straight games?
2. What is the old
name for spitball
pitchers?

ANSWERS
1. 1914.   2. Cuspidor curvers.

HUBBARD

Color T.V.

NOT EVEN A CONCEPT-ually innovative design could save Bowman from its inevitable, Topps-induced demise. Yet the revered enterprise out of Philadelphia forged ahead with its most

(Today's equivalent layout might be a mock Web site on a computer monitor.) An unusual segment of the roster was its 31 cards devoted to umpires, those often unsung arbiters of the baseball diamond. American League head of

1928, joined the major-league ranks in 1936, and worked nearly two decades' worth of A.L. games, with appearances in four World Series and three All-Star Games. Hubbard's large frame gave him a commanding on-field presence

1955 BOWMAN #315 — CAL HUBBARD

daring motif to date. As televisions became ubiquitous in American living rooms, and as baseball games were broadcast on those TVs, Bowman pro-jected its 320 subjects with the round-cornered screens, wooden borders, and knob-adorned control panels that fronted those massive, boxy, stand-alone units of the *Honeymooners* era.

umpires Cal Hubbard was perhaps the most interesting figure in the group. An elected member of both Canton's Pro Football Hall of Fame and Coopers-town's Baseball Hall of Fame, Hubbard was a star tackle for the world champion Green Bay Packers in the late 1920s and early 1930s. He began calling balls and strikes on the minor-league level in

and, although his card #315 begs recitation of the old line about umpires needing glasses, he also had extraordi-nary 20-10 vision in his prime. Bowman's inventive 1955 issue would be the company's last hurrah, marking the end of an influential tenure and unimpeachable legacy.
Estimated Value: $225

W HAT'S NOT TO love about this card? Topps covered all the bases with its flamboyant depiction of the Mick in his defining season of 1956. Mantle's smile more or less says

ing grab. A trio of cartoons on the back applauds Mantle's home run exploits and speed. One frame shows him motoring after a long fly, his legs a cloud of dust and his silhouette lamenting, "I'm his shadow and I can't keep up with

three more four-baggers in the World Series, most importantly the game-winning solo shot in Don Larsen's "Perfecto." Although the year's card #135 will never hold the allure or value of Mantle's 1952 Topps treasure,

1956 Topps #135 — Mickey Mantle

"Baseball's the greatest!," his Yankees cap symbolizes the franchise's storied success, his name and signature evoke boyhood awe, and his action pose forever freezes him in a dramatic game-saver.

him." No one could keep pace with Mantle in '56. His league-leading .353 average, 52 home runs, and 130 RBI were tantamount to the A.L. Triple Crown and MVP. Then Mantle clubbed

many aficionados still find the charismatic, horizontally aligned collectible superior on multiple levels.
Estimated Value: $2,500

THE ART DIRECTORS AT Topps could not have generated a more perfect tribute for Jackie Robinson's final season in the majors. In its second straight year of horizontal, twofold designs, the firm the printing press, the Dodgers were on the heels of their '55 championship, the long-awaited "Next Year" for which the Flatbush faithful had so famously pined. The following off-season, Robinson, hampered by knee problems, intimated in a magazine interview that he card #30 of 340 in Topps' 1956 issue, became the barrier-breaker's cherished farewell depiction. And a worthy homage it is. Robinson sweeps across home in a cloud of dust, his teammate Johnny Podres looking on as the slow-

1956 Topps #30 – Jackie Robinson

paired a winning portrait with a familiar scene from the fast-motion highlight reels of the day: Jackie stealing home. He would swipe home plate a total of 19 times in his decade-long career. Of course, Topps had no way of knowing that 1956 would prove to be Robinson's swan song; not even he himself could have foreseen the strange sequence of events that would end his prestigious tenure. When this card hit was ready to retire. The Brooklyn brass responded by unceremoniously shuffling him to the team's reviled crosstown rivals, the New York Giants, for $30,000 and pitcher Dick Littlefield. Perhaps to spite Dodger general manager Buzz Bavasi, Robinson turned down the Giants' hefty salary offer of $60,000 and succinctly retired as planned. Thus, this dynamic collectible, to-act catcher realizes he never had a chance anyway; Jackie's speed practically got him there before the pitch itself. Although the Dodger icon's playing days came to a thorny end, his cardboard gallery concluded with all of the dignity and elegance Robinson deserves.

Estimated Value: $470

BROOKLYN DODGERS

FRONT ROW: Shuba, Zimmer, Coach Becker, Coach Pitler, Manager Alston, Coach Herman, Reese, Howell, Amoros, Campanella. 2nd ROW: Griffin, Erskine, Koufax, Scott, Craig, Newcombe, Spooner, Hoak, Furillo, Kellert, Trainer Wendler. BACK ROW: Meyer, Gilliam, Loes, Labine, Hodges, Roebuck, Bessent, Snider, Podres, Walker, Robinson. Batboy Di Giovanna seated in front.

TEAM
TOPPS
166
CARD

BROOKLYN DODGERS

Last year Brooklyn won their first World Series with the team that the experts call the greatest in the Dodger history. In the early days Jake Daubert and Zack Wheat were the Dodger batting stars while the great "Dazzy" Vance averaged 17 wins per year in his 11 seasons as a Brooklyn hurler. "Dixie" Walker, Dolf Camilli and Pete Reiser were all leading N.L. batters and Fred Fitzsimmons, Kirby Higbe and Whitlow Wyatt were Dodger mound mainstays.

DODGERS' ALL TIME SEASON RECORDS		
MOST HITS	1654	1930
MOST HOME RUNS	208	1953
MOST STOLEN BASES	205	1904
HIGHEST BATTING AVERAGE	.304	1930
MOST DOUBLE PLAYS	192	1951
MOST GAMES WON	105	1953
MOST CONSECUTIVE GAMES WON	15	1924
MOST RUNS SCORED IN ONE GAME	25	1901

EBBETS FIELD
HOME OF THE DODGERS
SEATING CAPACITY: 32,111

PENNANT WINNING TEAMS—1916, 1920, 1941, 1947, 1949, 1952, 1953, 1955
WORLD CHAMPIONSHIP TEAM—1955

BE STILL THE BEATING hearts of Brooklynites. Here are the reigning champions that brought respect and honor to Flatbush in 1955, the long-awaited "Next Year" that fans had sought throughout the Yankees' postwar glory days. Dem Bums were bums no more, and their proud smiles of satisfaction and retribution populate the 33-man lineup disseminated in Topps' 1956 edition. Topps had issued a small, stand-alone set of black-and-white team images in 1951, but the 16 cards of five years later marked the company's first foray into the team-card subsets that would become a staple of future issues. Ten of the sixteen inaugural entries were released in the single version seen above, with team name centered left to right and no visible denotation of "1955." The remaining six—Cubs, Phillies, Indians, Redlegs, Braves, and Orioles—came three different ways: dated "1955" next to the team name; undated with the team name centered; and undated with the team name left-justified. It's reasonable to assume that the new subset was initially less popular than the familiar, individual-player images, and that many team cards may have even been thrown away with wrappers and checklists. To be sure, Yankee fans enjoyed getting rid of the Dodgers card, and vice versa once the Yanks exacted their World Series revenge in '56.

Estimated Value: $550

1956 Topps #166 Team Card — Brooklyn Dodgers

RANK ROBINSON'S rookie card coincided with the dawning of a new era for Topps. The company had previously relied on hand-colored black-and-white photos for its baseball sets. Now, each

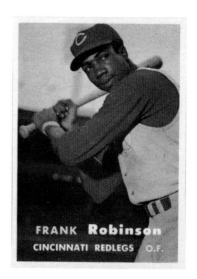

cinnati outfielder had pummeled N.L. pitching for 38 home runs, 83 RBI, and a league-best 122 runs scored. He was a natural choice for Rookie of the Year, and within five years would add MVP hardware to his expanding trophy case.

1957 Topps #35 — Frank Robinson

depiction employed true-to-life full-color photography. Another innovation revolved around the cards' reverses: for the first time, Topps listed the respective player's complete lifetime statistics. As a sophomore, Robinson's stats were only one line long—but they spoke volumes. The 21-year-old Cin-

Even greater success came when Robinson joined the Baltimore Orioles in 1966. He immediately won his second Most Valuable Player award, this time in the A.L., and he remains the only player to win baseball's highest honor in both leagues. Four pennants and two championships later, Robinson

returned to Ohio with the Cleveland Indians, where he made history as the first-ever black manager in the majors.
Estimated Value: $750

OPPS SAVED THE BEST for last in its 1957 release. Who better to round out the much-touted gallery than Mick and Yogi? The pinstriped pair had combined for 82 regular-season homers and 6

that if Ruth's 60 Homer mark is to be topped, the muscular Oklahoman will do it." The summary also likens Mantle and Berra to the Murderers' Row lineup of Ruth and Gehrig's prime. In the frontal dugout shot, both Bronx

1957 Topps #407 "Yankees' Power Hitters" — Mantle/Berra

World Series four-baggers in 1956, plus laid claim to four of the last six MVP awards. Mantle, coming off his Triple Crown campaign, is described by Topps' card-back biographers as "one of the all time long ball hitters," adding, mistakenly as it were, "Experts figure

Bombers smile with bats in hand and with two teammates lounging in the background. Multi-player cards from the issue's scarce 4th Series were a hallmark of 1957 Topps, as were the spectacular photography, the final *Brooklyn* Dodgers and *New York*

Giants inclusions, and the debuts of up-and-comers Frank Robinson, Rocky Colavito, Don Drysdale, and—Yankee fans beware—Bill Mazeroski.
Estimated Value: $1,350

Roger Maris

OUTFIELD   CLEVELAND INDIANS

ROGER MARIS   After attending the University of Minnesota, Rog broke into baseball with Fargo in 1953. His consistantly high batting marks won him rapid promotions. After hitting .293 at Indianapolis, he joined the Tribe.

BEFORE JOINING CLEVELAND, ROG HAD A .303 MINOR LEAGUE AVERAGE.

IN 1954, AT KEOKUK, HE BELTED 32 HOMERS AND DROVE IN 111 RUNS!

Height: 6'
Weight: 197
Bats: Left
Throws: Right
Home: North Fargo, N. D.
Born: Sept. 10, 1934

MAJOR & MINOR* LEAGUE BATTING RECORD									FIELDING			
	Games	AB	Runs	Hits	2B	3B	HR	RBI	B.Avg	PO	A	E	F.Avg
YEAR	116	358	61	84	9	5	14	51	.235	266	10	7	.975
LIFE*	517	1817	339	550	80	30	78	353	.303	976	62	44	.959

GLIMPSING ROGER MARIS in any uniform other than Yankee threads can be disconcerting. The trademark high-cut sleeves are there, as are the gritty James Dean-like features, but where are the pinstripes? Like "Shoeless Joe" Jackson a half-century earlier, Maris started making a name for himself in Cleveland before landing with the team that would come to define his career. His first full season in the majors, 1958 saw the outfielder establish himself as a legitimate power hitter. He spent the first third of the year with the Tribe, and the latter two-thirds with the Athletics (another of Jackson's early teams, though by the mid-1950s they had moved from Philadelphia to Kansas City). Maris swatted 28 home runs and plated 80 base runners, drawing the attention of All-Star balloters and Yankee executives alike. Once he was traded to the "Bronx Bombers" in late 1959, the Minnesota native more than lived up to the team's nickname. He hit 100 round-trippers and 254 RBI in the two-year span of 1960-61, highlighted by his record-breaking "61 in '61" campaign. The fermentation of those skills started back in '58, the year young fans got their first peek at the rising star on this orange-accented collectible from Topps' vibrant 494-subject set. Apparently, the road from Cleveland travels many places...but not to

1958 Topps #47 — Roger Maris

Cooperstown. Despite two MVP awards, one Gold Glove, three World Series championships, and, of course, nearly four decades' occupancy of the single-season home run title, Roger Maris—like his Cleveland forebear Joe Jackson—does not yet have a plaque at the Baseball Hall of Fame.
Estimated Value: $700

Hank Aaron
OUTFIELD—MILWAUKEE BRAVES

**JOIN THE
HIRES BASEBALL
CLUB TODAY!**

Learn how to play baseball from
the BIG LEAGUERS! How to pitch!
Catch! Judge plays! Just paste
10c to the Hires bottle cap picture on the reverse side and send
with 2 Hires bottle caps to:

CHARLES E. HIRES COMPANY
P. O. Box 500, Haddonfield, New Jersey

LOOK WHAT YOU GET:

1 Hires "How To Play
   Baseball Book".
2 Valuable membership card.

Printed in U. S. A.

Hank Aaron
MILWAUKEE BRAVES

To: HIRES BASEBALL CLUB
    BOX 500
    HADDONFIELD, NEW JERSEY

YOUR NAME

ADDRESS

CITY AND STATE

IT'S A WONDER THAT ANY OF these cards have survived with their perforated tabs intact. Besides the fact that the tabs were delicately fitted into slots on six-pack cartons of root beer, they also doubled as mail-in examples a rare sight today, indeed. Pictured here is one of the very best. The edges are sharp, the colors are luminous, and the surface betrays no heavy handling or soda stains. Hank Aaron looks to be on top of the world— Hammerin' Hank launched 3 home runs, plated 7 runners, and batted a scintillating .393 in the series. 1958 brought another trip to the Fall Classic, and again the Braves and Yanks went the distance. This time, it was the Bronx

1958 HIRES ROOT BEER #44 — HANK AARON

tickets for membership in the Hires Baseball Club. One way or another, most of the appendages were severed from the "knothole" view of their players, making damage-free, full-size and he was. At the start of '58, Aaron was the reigning N.L. MVP and his Braves were unlikely champions, having prevailed over the Yankees in a seven-game World Series battle. Bombers who would triumph behind a quartet of homers by outfielder Hank Bauer, who had belted a mere dozen round-trippers all season long.
Estimated Value: $650

HARMON KILLEBREW
WASHINGTON SENATORS

THE CONCEPT WAS brilliant. Take two of the game's premier power-hitters, put them in an empty ballpark (Gladiator-style, *mano a mano*), give them a practice pitcher serving up fat ones over the plate, set the TV cameras rolling, and let the rocket-launching begin. In the inaugural season of the short-lived show *Home Run Derby*, hosted by broadcaster Mark Scott, nineteen players took their cuts in weekly nine-inning battles—future Hall of Famers Mickey Mantle, Al Kaline, Harmon Killebrew, Duke Snider, Hank Aaron, Willie Mays, Ernie Banks, Frank Robinson, and Ed Mathews, as well as less-celebrated sluggers Rocky Colavito, Jackie Jensen, Ken Boyer, Bob Cerv, Bob Allison, Gil Hodges, Wally Post, Dick Stuart, Gus Triandos, and Jim Lemon. The contest gave rise to a spin-off card set whose limited original distribution now precludes many hobbysts' hopes of set completion. Killebrew, in his first full season with the Washington Senators, sports the issue's fiercest facial expression, as if "Killer" might well crush the next pitch clear to China. *Home Run Derby* took place in L.A.'s ivy-less Wrigley Field, built by gum magnate Phillip K. Wrigley in the 1920s to house the Los Angeles Angels of the Pacific Coast League. A longstanding Hollywood locale, the stadium had previously hosted scenes in such classic baseball films as *The Pride of the Yankees* (1942), *The Winning Team* (1952), *The Pride of St. Louis* (1952), and *Damn Yankees* (1958). *Estimated Value: $500*

1959 HOME RUN DERBY — HARMON KILLEBREW

THE CARDINALS' 6-FOOT-1 rookie right-hander raised high expectations from the start and never failed to exceed them. Bob Gibson was the complete package: a fireballer foremost but with the versatil-

since. Consider: Two Cy Young Awards (1968, 1970); five 20-win seasons; nine Gold Glove trophies (1965-1973); and 24 career home runs at the plate. His 1968 campaign was something of a "perfect storm" for opposing

straight in the "W" column), a 17-strikeout Game 1 in '68, and, from the batter's box, a pair of round-trippers and 3 RBI. Fans outside St. Louis had gotten their first look at "Hoot" on this pleasing, pink-infused collectible from Topps'

1959 Topps #514 – Bob Gibson

ity of a one-man band. He had been a collegiate basketball standout, even netting a season with the Harlem Globetrotters, and his natural athleticism—combined with an unflappable competitive spirit—infused every facet of his play on the diamond. Gibson pitched, fielded, and batted about as well as any moundsman before or

hitters, as Gibson logged 22 victories, 13 shutouts, 268 strikeouts, and a miniscule 1.12 ERA, the lowest earned run average since Dutch Leonard in 1914. For all his regular-season successes, Gibson invariably stepped up his performance come October. A trio of 1960s World Series saw him hurl nine total wins (including a record seven

final release of the 1950s. His depiction maintains a status as the set's premier rookie card, and—because of its late distribution in the issue's disproportionately off-centered 7th Series—as one of its condition and population rarities as well.

Estimated Value: $575

Roy Campanella is honored on May 7, 1959 at a
benefit game between the Yankees and Dodgers

SYMBOL OF COURAGE

ROY CAMPANELLA

550 SYMBOL OF COURAGE

Roy Campanella truly is a symbol of courage,
not only to baseball but to persons in all walks
of life. Roy's fighting comeback from the tragic
automobile accident which threatened to make
him a total invalid, and his cheerfulness through
it all, have been an inspiration to everyone. It
is the same example of courage, faith and spirit
which made him a great catcher. Any young
man who has ambitions to become a baseball
player, will do well to pattern after Campanella's all-out effort whether he was winning or
losing in a baseball game or fighting against
great odds in a hospital. We, in the National
League, greatly miss "Campy" on the playing
field but are delighted to see him back in action
as a coach with the Dodgers. Everyone wishes
Roy the very best of everything in his courageous fight.

Warren Giles

WARREN GILES, PRES. • NATIONAL LEAGUE

O N OPENING DAY 1958, after the beloved Bums had left Flatbush for L.A.'s palm trees and tropical clime, one name was noticeably, painfully absent from the roster. Duke Snider, Pee Wee Reese, accident in early 1958 confined him to a wheelchair for life—but it did not cripple his spirit. Campanella would arrive in the City of Angels as a coach and, in turn, a courageous role model. Topps devoted the 550th of 572 cards in its of 1951 had now become the authorita-tive voice for a generation of young hob-byists. With #550, Topps channeled its considerable influence toward con-sciousness-raising by shining a light on Campy's condition and bravery, instead

1959 Topps #550 "Symbol of Courage" — Roy Campanella

Gil Hodges, Don Drysdale, and Sandy Koufax all suited up for their new phase out west. The missing man was three-time MVP and unwavering team leader Roy Campanella, whose last major-league appearance had come, unbe-knownst to anyone at the time, in the final game at Ebbets Field, on September 24, 1957. A near-fatal auto 1959 set to Campy. The front pictures him smiling broadly in spite of the tragic circumstances; the reverse provides stirring praise written by National League President Warren Giles. This final Topps issue of the 1950s showed the company's maturation throughout the "Golden Age" decade. The indus-try's ambitious, inexperienced upstart of succumbing to the period's prevail-ing taboos about physical handicaps. Campanella lived a long, proud life after his injury. He was enshrined with a Hall of Fame plaque in 1969 and died on June 26, 1993.
Estimated Value: $330

Jan. 23, 1959 — Ted Signs For 1959

#68
COLLECT
ALL 80

BASEBALL'S GREATEST
Ted Williams

Ted signed his 1959 contract in Boston for a reported $125,000. He has been baseball's highest paid player for several years. Twenty years have passed since Ted first started playing for the Boston Red Sox. Ted feels great and said that he's "going to play a lot more this year than people think I will".

All Card Data by E. Mifflin   Wide World Photo

"Bucky" Harris, Bosox General Manager, and Williams at contract signing in Boston.

FLEER DEVOTED AN entire 80-card edition to Ted Williams in the American hero's penultimate season of 1959. Williams had long been a source of dispute between the competing card compa- the most clout, money, and resources. Fleer would have been hard-pressed to produce a standard issue that could compete with that of the Topps machine, so a specialty set—one with the Splendid Splinter!—was an ideal haunted the pictures of Williams with Babe Ruth, Jim Thorpe, Joe Cronin, or Jimmie Foxx, and so #68 alone remains the issue's key acquisition for collectors. On the field, Williams had an off-year in 1959. He returned to form for

1959 FLEER TED WILLIAMS #68
"TED SIGNS FOR 1959" — TED WILLIAMS

nies that vied for permission to use his image. The decision to now endorse an all-Ted-all-the-time set must have been a charitable gesture on Williams' part. It was also an unlikely coup in the card industry. Topps, having officially dispensed with early rival Bowman, had alternative. Interestingly, a copyright controversy arose that was unrelated to Williams himself. Card #68, "Ted Signs for 1959," was pulled from the printing press for depicting Red Sox General Manager Bucky Harris without Harris' consent. No such problems his much-touted final season in 1960, batting .316 and socking 29 home runs—the 29th coming in the last at-bat of his vaunted career.
Estimated Value: $900

WILLIE MAYS
OUTFIELD   SAN. FRAN. GIANTS

WHAT WOULD IN-spire Topps, parent company of Bazooka-brand gum, to cast aside its scruples and print 1959 Bazooka cards on the *underside* of 20-count display boxes for "Big Twin

clientele on a new, more pricey endorphin dependency—box-buying. A predictable pitfall was the damage caused by both countertop friction at the candy shop and poor aptitude at home in cutting cardboard along dotted lines with-

stymied set-builders intent on a high-caliber assembly. Regarding Mays, "Say Hey" was then in his second season since the New York Giants' migration to San Francisco. He had adapted quickly to the Bay Area, averaging 32

1959 Bazooka — Willie Mays

Chews"? What cognitive dissonance permitted the Topps brass to condone its subsidiary's multi-sport cards as uncut panels placed directly on the box and, moreover, on the box's most vulnerable surface? Presumably, the Bazooka rubric was intended to circumvent pack-buying and hook its young

out mangling the desired card. An unanticipated foible was the temptation for buyers to scour the visible bottom panels in order to seek out their favorites among the 23 players: Hank Aaron, Ernie Banks, Rocky Colavito, Mickey Mantle, Willie Mays. These variables in condition and availability have

homers, 100 RBI and a .330 average at the plate, while demonstrating in Candlestick Park's vast expanses that his throwing arm was still, one might say, as powerful as a bazooka.
Estimated Value: $1,500

That gritty breakfast cereal known as Grape-Nuts has taken a lot of guff over the decades. Chief among the grievances are perhaps these three: The cereal actually contains no grapes, there are

hobby would be without its 1960 series of "Post Sports Stars," which was available exclusively on the box-back of that very cereal beloved by diabetic and geriatric populations. Nine heroes of baseball, football, and basketball—

dents, and casual blemishes from enthusiastic handling has considerably thinned the amount of available gems. Condition aside, Post Sports Stars were savored by cereal-lovers and collectors for their unique visuals: the illustrated

1960 Post Cereal — Mickey Mantle

no nuts either, and, above all, the texture calls to mind a tooth-cracking gravel driveway. (*Saturday Night Live* memorably parodied the Post product in a commercial sketch for freshly mined "Quarry" cereal.) If it weren't for Grape-Nuts, however, the card-collecting

Mickey Mantle, Don Drysdale, Al Kaline, Eddie Mathews, Harmon Killebrew, Johnny Unitas, Frank Gifford, Bob Cousy, and Bob Pettit— were printed in blazing colors with cut-along-the-dotted-line perimeters. The combination of shelf wear, scissor acci-

faux-wood frame and shiny plaque, the picture of a much-admired athlete, and the brilliant backdrop—in Mantle's case, bubble-gum pink.
Estimated Value: $2,500

FOR ITS OPENING SET OF the new decade, the Topps Company—or, rather, Topps' anonymous "Youth of America" committee—devoted a specialty card to first baseman Willie McCovey. This, plus up the sort of numbers managers hope for from an April-to-September rookie. Take Day One for instance: McCovey makes up for lost time by going 4-for-4 against the Philadelphia Phillies, with a pair of triples off ace Robin Roberts. In his Ted Williams-matching total of 521 homers stands as a crowning achievement. He is perhaps the most underrated member of the "500 Home Run Club," in part because his feats were often overshadowed by teammate

1960 Topps #316 "All-Star Rookie" — Willie McCovey

National League Rookie of the Year honors, despite McCovey's having played in a mere 54 games the previous season. How could the smooth-swinging Giant have proven so much in just one-third of a full major league campaign, starting so late as July 30, to warrant such fanfare? Namely by putting mid-August, McCovey starts a 22-game hitting streak. He finishes the year with 13 four-baggers, 38 RBI, and a sizzling .354 average. Had he suited up for the whole season, McCovey might well have added MVP hardware to his expanding trophy case. "Stretch" soon developed into a power hitter, and Willie Mays. 1969 was an exception, though, as McCovey lit up National League pitching for 45 dingers and 126 RBI, and socked two more over the wall in the All-Star Game—capturing both the N.L. and A.S. MVP awards. *Estimated Value: $325*

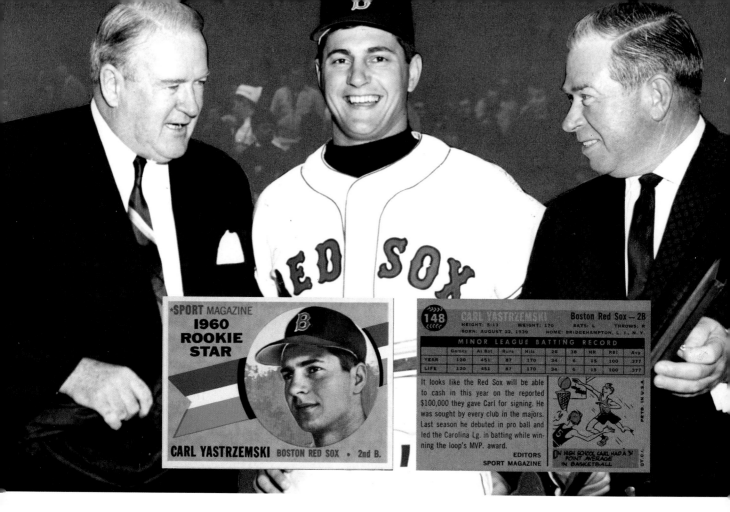

EIGHTEEN ALL-STAR Games, seven Gold Glove Awards, three batting titles, and a Triple-Crown MVP season, yet "Yaz" still eludes the echelon of Mantle, Mays, and Aaron. Fact is, Yastrzemski, Yastrzemski were his lack of a big-league championship (compared with Mantle's seven titles) and his 48-homer deficiency for membership in the "500 Home Run Club" (source of commemorative prints and promotional signings Yastrzemski his due from the start, including him in its 572-card 1960 edition before he ever took the field. His *Sport Magazine* "Rookie Star" selection remains as underestimated as the Hall of Famer himself, about whom outfield-

1960 TOPPS #148 "ROOKIE STAR" —
CARL YASTRZEMSKI

like his peer Harmon Killebrew, emerged too late to claim membership in that Golden Age of the fifties. Baseball simply wasn't as important to Americans in the Vietnam era of the sixties and seventies as it was in the decade of Spam, Jell-O, and *The Honeymooners*. Also working against *ad infinitum*). The less-exclusive "3,000 Hit Club" evidently doesn't hold the same powers of immortality, even if Yaz's 3,419 lifetime safeties still stand as seventh-best all-time. During 23 seasons, the bastion of Beantown also played in more games (3,308) than any other American Leaguer. Topps gave er Joe Lahoud once said, "Yaz did it all the time. We'd be on the road and he'd call, 'C'mon, we're going to the ballpark.' I'd say, 'Christ, it's only one o'clock. The game's at seven.' He lived, breathed, ate, and slept baseball."
Estimated Value: $450

Mazeroski is congratulated with a firm pinch after his historic Game 7 homer.

1960 WORLD SERIES

GAME #7

Mazeroski's Homer Wins It!

312 GAME #7—1960 WORLD SERIES

HOW THE YANKEES SCORED:
5TH INNING: Skowron homered. ONE RUN.
6TH INNING: Richardson singled. Kubek walked. Face came in. Mantle singled, scoring Richardson and sending Kubek to third. Berra homered, Mantle and Kubek scoring. FOUR RUNS.
8TH INNING: Berra walked. Skowron singled. Blanchard singled, scoring Berra. Boyer doubled, scoring Skowron. TWO RUNS.
9TH INNING: Richardson singled. Long pinch-hit and singled. Mantle singled, scoring Richardson. McDougald ran for Long, Berra grounded out, scoring McDougald TWO RUNS.

HOW THE PIRATES SCORED:
1ST INNING: Skinner walked. Nelson homered. TWO RUNS.
2ND INNING: Burgess singled. Hoak walked. Mazeroski bunt singled to load the bases. Virdon singled to score two Mazeroski. TWO RUNS.
8TH INNING: Cimoli singled. Virdon singled when the ball took a bad hop and struck Kubek in the stomach. Clemente got an infield hit, Virdon scoring, scoring Groat and Clemente ahead of him. FIVE RUNS.
9TH INNING: Mazeroski homered to win the series. ONE RUN.

YANKEE PITCHERS: Turley, Stafford (2), Shantz (3), Coates (8), Terry (8). PIRATE PITCHERS: Law, Face (6), Friend (9), Haddix (9). WINNER: HADDIX. LOSER: TERRY.

NEW YORK   0 0 0 0 1 4 0 2 2—9
PITTSBURGH 2 2 0 0 0 0 0 5 1—10
T.C.G. PRINTED IN U.S.A.

THE JUBILANT SCENE OF Pirates hero Bill Mazeroski swarmed by teammates and fans as he crossed home plate at Forbes Field made the front page of newspapers nationwide. A season later, Topps featured the iconic image in its "1960 World Series" subset. Young collectors clamored for card #312. Here was the man who had usurped the Yankees' perennial throne in fairy-tale fashion, belting Ralph Terry's 1-0 slider over the left-field fence for the first World Series-winning home run in baseball history. With that one swing, Mazeroski's Pirates overcame a lop-sided 29-run deficit in the 7-game series—26 runs to the Yankees' 55— and brought home a long-overdue championship to the Steel City. The blast was just Mazeroski's thirteenth of the year, and one of only 140 homers in his entire 17 seasons of play. Defense was Maz's specialty, as attested by the second-sacker's eight Gold Glove Awards. Mazeroski was inducted to Cooperstown in 2001, around the same time *The Sporting News* selected his walk-off homer as the Number 2 event—second only to Bobby Thomson's "Shot Heard Round the World"—in the magazine's list of Baseball's 25 Greatest Moments. *Estimated Value: $50*

1961 Topps #312 "1960 World Series" — Bill Mazeroski

Maris clouts number 61.

TOPPS 2	ROGER MARIS					N. Y. Yankees, outfield					

HT: 6'0" WT: 195 BATS: LEFT THROWS: RIGHT
BORN: SEPTEMBER 10 1934 HOME: RAYTOWN, MO

COMPLETE MAJOR AND MINOR LEAGUE BATTING RECORD

YEAR	TEAM	LEA.	G	AB	R	H	2B	3B	HR	RBI	AVG.
1953	Fargo-Moorhead	North.	114	418	74	136	18	13	9	80	.325
1954	Keokuk	I. I. I.	134	502	105	158	26	6	32	111	.315
1955	Tulsa	Texan	25	90	9	21	1	0	1	9	.233
1955	Reading	East.	113	374	74	108	15	3	19	78	.289
1956	Indianapolis	A. A.	131	433	77	127	20	8	17	75	.293
1957	Cleveland	A. L.	116	358	61	84	9	5	14	51	.235
1958	Cleveland-K. C.	A. L.	150	583	87	140	19	4	28	80	.240
1959	Kansas City	A. L.	122	433	69	118	21	7	16	72	.273
1960	New York	A. L.	136	499	98	141	18	7	39	112	.283
Major League Totals		4 Yrs.	524	1873	315	483	67	23	97	315	.258

Roger had a tremendous season in 1960 with the New York Yankees. During the 1960 World Series he hit 2 homers against Pittsburgh. Roger Maris was named the Most Valuable Player in the A.L. for 1960.

ROGER MARIS
Outfield   New York Yankees

BY VIRTUE OF HIS 1960 A.L. MVP honors, Roger Maris merited the #2 slot in Topps' 1961 set. N.L. MVP Dick Groat occupied card #1, no doubt because Groat's Pittsburgh Pirates (not Maris' New York Yankees) were defending world champions—thanks to Bill Mazeroski's championship-clinching clout. In '61, the pendulum of diamond glory would swing back to the junior circuit, back to the Yankees, back to the "M & M Boys," and, ultimately, back to Maris. The taciturn outfielder dug his heels in all season long to do the unthinkable: eclipse Babe Ruth's long-ball record from that other majestic year in pinstripe history, 1927. Maris withstood media pressure. He surmounted the asterisk-obsessed detractors, the Ruth devotees, the Mantle mavens. He summoned that inner sanctum of strength that pulsates inside superior athletes, the wellspring that fueled Joe DiMaggio's "Streak," Ted Williams' .400 season, and Don Larsen's Perfect Game. Maris negated the skeptics and validated the believers by clocking number 61 when it counted most—the last day of the season. His almost-mythic year was yet an improbable speck of stardust in destiny's haze when Maris took second billing in Topps'

1961 Topps #2 – Roger Maris

1961 release. He would soon prove to the world and to himself that, with all due respect to the Sultan of Swat, second place simply wouldn't do. Maris was no regent to the Single-Season Home Run throne; he would be king.

Estimated Value: $575

HANK AARON
Right Field National League

For the first time in 6 years Hank dipped below the .300 mark in 1960. Still, he had the kind of a season that other ballplayers dream of. The Braves' rightfielder blistered the ball for a .292 batting average and socked 40 four-baggers. Hank knocked home 112 runs and was one of the games best clutch hitters. Twice the Yankees have been misfortunate enough to meet Aaron in World Series competition. He has slammed New York pitching for a .364 average in 55 at bats. Hank is a spectacular gloveman in the outfield, having won several awards for his defensive ability. The rightfielder won his first N.L. batting crown in 1956 (.328) and followed with another title in 1959 (.355).

© T.C. G.—PRTD. IN U.S.A.

XTRA, EXTRA, READ ALL *about it! Aaron plays in seventh mid-summer classic!* Topps teamed up with *The Sporting News* for its high-number series of All-Star cards. Hank Aaron and his fellow newspaper-busting standouts concluded the gum company's then-largest offering of 587 images, an issue stocked with special subsets like "All-Star," "Baseball Thrills," and "World Series," as well as numerous cameos by Mickey Mantle and Roger Maris. The M & M Boys' onslaught against Ruth's 60-home-run record was the story of the year (not to mention the decade and half century), making Topps seem all the wiser for Mick and Roger's abundant representation in the '61 set. Meanwhile, Hammerin' Hank meted out another rock-solid campaign, batting at a .328 clip with 34 homers and 120 RBI. He also paced the league in doubles (39) and, for the third straight year, total bases (358).
Estimated Value: $250

1961 Topps #577 "All-Star" — Hank Aaron

A TEST ISSUE, TOPPS' "Dice Game" numbered 18 cards, none of which ever saw the light of distribution. The experimental set was scrapped after preliminary production, despite the fact that it offered unique player images and, on the reverse, a creative matrix of batting outcomes based on dice rolls and four varieties of pitches. Attribution to Topps, in lieu of any overt copyright line, is rooted in the set's status as an unreleased test issue, as well as on the design and font of the caption box. Mickey Mantle, Willie Mays, and Stan Musial command the highest premiums, with Mantle—fewer than a handful of whose depictions are thought to exist—ranking by far as the most desirable member of the trio. Adding more luster to the card's scarcity and intrigue is its origin in that magical year of 1961, when Mantle's career high of 54 homers was bested by Roger Maris' record-breaking 61 round-trippers. In his smiling pose on this rarest of all Mantle cards, the Commerce Comet appears optimistic about his odds in the upcoming season's home run race. But, as he would soon find out, the die was already cast. *Estimated Value: $25,000*

1961 Topps Dice Game — Mickey Mantle

I N APRIL 1962, READERS OF *LIFE* delved into the magazine's newest issue (its cover showcasing Elizabeth Taylor and Richard Burton on the set of *Cleopatra*) and in a series of three similarly designed editions spanning 1961 to 1963. Although hardly rivaling Topps' success, the cereal-maker's sets nevertheless earned a following for their profusion of top players. For the 1962 release, 200 different cards were issued on the back panels of cereal boxes, with American Leaguers occupying numbers 1-100 and National Leaguers spanning 101-200. Only the popular M & M Boys appeared in that 1962 issue of *LIFE*—doubtless because of their home-run heroics the previous year. Most readers removed

1962 POST CEREAL #5 AND #6
LIFE MAGAZINE INSERT —
MICKEY MANTLE/ROGER MARIS

came across a pleasant surprise. Post Cereal had reserved space for a promotional insert with Mickey Mantle on one side and Roger Maris on the other. The card images hailed from Post's second sion of top players. For the 1962 release, 200 different cards were issued on the back panels of cereal boxes, with American Leaguers occupying numbers 1-100 and National the double-sided insert, but it is still possible to locate copies with the advertising freebie intact.
Estimated Value: $250

THE CHICAGO CUBS' "Curse of the Billy Goat" strikes again. Cubs management made its most disastrous trade in franchise history in 1964, shuffling prospect Lou Brock to the St. Louis tavern owner William "Billy Goat" Sianis bought two tickets for Game 4 of the 1945 World Series at Wrigley Field, and he brought his pet goat Murphy for the second seat as something of a good-luck charm. Denied entrance at point Sianis sent Wrigley a telegram reading, "Who stinks now?") and have not returned to the World Series ever since. Now back to the Brock-Broglio imbroglio. Card #387 in Topps' 1962 edition pictures the Cubs rookie in a

1962 Topps #387 — Lou Brock

Cardinals for former 20-game-winner Ernie Broglio. The long and short of it (literally) is that Brock played 16 seasons for the Cards and amassed over 3,000 career hits while Broglio was out of the gate (or ejected mid-game, depending on the account), Sianis requested that Cubs owner Phillip K. Wrigley address the matter himself. Wrigley decreed that the goat could not enter serene, static portrait, so very different from the outfielder's eventual reputation for constant motion, fleet agility, and lightning speed. The Hall of Famer's 938 lifetime steals and record-

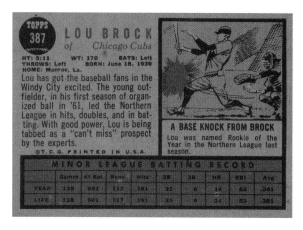

baseball within three years, having posted just seven victories since the exchange. The kicker of course was Brock's subsequent two world championships in St. Louis, as opposed to the Cubs' ongoing championship drought since 1908 and pennant void since 1945—the ominous year of Murphy the Goat. So the story goes, Chicago the "Friendly Confines" because of the animal's barnyard odor. Sianis left with his hoofed companion in tow, but not before angrily wishing a hex against the Cubs' future championship hopes so long as Murphy the Goat was barred from Wrigley Field. Needless to say, the "Lovable Losers" dropped Game 4 and the '45 Series altogether (at which setting 118 in 1974 alone ushered in a new dawn of base-swiping in the majors. To this day, the National League's annual trophy for stolen-base leader bears his name, the Lou Brock Award.
Estimated Value: $340

WILLIE, MICKEY, and...hey, where's the Duke? Well, two out of three still a "Managers' Dream" do make— and Hank Aaron in the background amply suffices in Duke Snider's on the card-back sidesteps Roger Maris' gargantuan feat of 1961 in deference to Mantle's legacy: "Mickey threatened Ruth's home run record last season, but injuries spoiled his bid." In 1962, Mays bested his centerfield

MANAGERS' DREAM
MICKEY MANTLE • WILLIE MAYS

1962 Topps #18 "Managers' Dream" — Mantle/Mays

absence. It had been five years since Mantle and Mays both called the Big Apple home, but Mays' migration west had no effect on their shared status as the game's most popular superstars. The powers-that-be at Topps certainly agreed. Observe how the description counterpart Mantle in four-baggers (49) and RBI (141), but the Mick one-upped him in batting average (.321) and, yes, another Yankee championship. Their appearance together came early in Topps' wood-bordered release, complete at 598 cards, and

#18 has not lost any of its luster in the intervening 44 years.
Estimated Value: $550

CONDITION STICKLERS may bemoan the full-bleed bottom banner so susceptible to flecks of border wear, but hobbyists oriented toward design and aesthetics tend to promulgate the 1963 set as one hues and unusually bright photographs, while Topps' lawyers mounted a defense of the gum company's inviolable, contractual right to certain ballplayers' images, to the detriment of its competitors. Little surprise, then,

POWER PLUS
Ernie Banks • Hank Aaron

1963 Topps #242 "Power Plus" — Banks/Aaron

of Topps' finest offerings. At the time of production, Topps executives knew the stakes were unusually high. Both Fleer and Post were viably testing the firm's dominion for the first time since Bowman had folded its tent in 1955. Topps rose to the challenge on both the production end and the legal front. Its art directors created an immense, star-saturated issue replete with dazzling that Fleer and Post were absent from the card scene in 1964 as the Topps steam-engine rolled on. This brilliant, quasi-candid shot of National League sluggers Ernie Banks and Hank Aaron exemplifies the best of what Topps had to offer with its 576-card tour de force. The previous season, Mr. Cub had tallied his sixth 35-plus-homer campaign, and Hammerin' Hank had belted 45 base-circling blasts, a career high. Card #242 celebrated their high-octane "Power Plus," and in so doing, highlighted two of the game's most upstanding ambassadors and true class-acts.
Estimated Value: $200

Rose hits number 4192 to surpass Ty Cobb as the all-time hits leader.

1963 ROOKIE STARS

PEDRO GONZALEZ
N. Y. YANKEES, 2B

KEN McMULLEN
L. A. DODGERS, 3B

PETE ROSE
CINCINNATI REDS, 2B

AL WEIS
CHI. WHITE SOX, SS

| 537 | 1963 ROOKIE STARS |

MINOR LEAGUE LIFETIME RECORDS

	G	AB	R	H	2B	3B	HR	RBI	AVG.
PEDRO GONZALEZ N. Y. YANKEES—2B	595	2286	364	695	96	25	34	269	.304
KEN McMULLEN L. A. DODGERS—3B	281	1022	186	291	54	8	42	177	.285
PETE ROSE CIN. REDS—2B	354	1345	301	427	59	52	12	191	.317
AL WEIS CHI. WHITE SOX—SS	472	1870	314	497	59	18	15	159	.266

© T.C.G. PRINTED IN U.S.A.

*I*S IT ANY WONDER THAT PETE Rose is the only one smiling among this freshman foursome? The Cincinnati native was manning second base for his hometown team en route to Rookie of the Year accolades of the four figures, their circular frames were red lights on the road to diamond immortality; for Rose, red meant zooming through the intersection Charlie Hustle-style, pedal-to-the-metal with the reckless abandon of one of his day, garnering publicity tantamount to his playing days for the Baseball Hall of Fame's ongoing kibosh on his enshrinement. Whether batting, running, sliding, fielding, or gambling, he has pushed himself to the extreme. Rose always

1963 Topps #537 "Rookie Stars" — Pete Rose

and, 22 years farther down the road, coronation as the "All-Time Hit King." His compatriots for the most part have disappeared into the ether, with the exception of shortstop Al Weis, thanks to card #537's tongue-in-cheek appellation as "The Al Weis Rookie." For three head-first slides. The scintillating first-year collectible remains the hallmark of its 576-card issue, despite appearances by such veterans as Mantle, Koufax, Mays, Aaron, and Clemente. From Day One, Rose was an irrepressible force—and he remains so to this understood his sensational, if checkered destiny. That's why he was smiling back in '63, and why his Cheshire-like grin still lingers today.
Estimated Value: $1,650

*I*N ORDER TO CIRCUMVENT Topps' litigious, monopolistic practices, Fleer resorted to marketing its 1963 set without the standard kid bait of bubble gum. The Topps juggernaut had succeeded in ostensibly staking an exclusive claim to player images on gum cards. Hence, there was only one way for David to have even a slingshot's chance against Goliath: Fleer eschewed bubble gum and chose another sugary temptation—cookies. The half-baked experiment proved a one-year, 66-card (plus unnumbered checklist) success, one of the few notable challenges to the post-Bowman supremacy of Topps. Willie Mays, Roberto Clemente, and Brooks Robinson headlined the issue, but the centerpiece turned out to be rising star Sandy Koufax. The southpaw won pitching's version of the Triple Crown

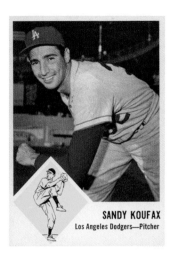

SANDY KOUFAX
Los Angeles Dodgers—Pitcher

1963 Fleer #42 — Sandy Koufax

with a league-leading 25 wins, 306 strikeouts, and 1.88 ERA. He then tossed a pair of complete-game victories in the Dodgers' World Series sweep of the Yankees. Koufax's performance translated to the Cy Young Award, National League MVP, and World Series MVP. He smiles warmly, with his pitching arm extended in full follow-through, on card #42 (a legendary Flatbush uniform number, no less). The '63 Fleer production led Topps to clamp down even harder on the legal ramifications of its player-permission contracts, forcing Fleer's plans for a follow-up set to crumble like one of its cookies. *Estimated Value: $350*

---

*F*OR TWO SEASONS IN the early sixties, Ken Hubbs brought a spark to the "Friendly Confines" of Wrigley Field. He was a ballhawk at second base from the get-go, his record-setting 78 straight errorless games in 1962 earning both Rookie of the Year and Gold Glove honors—the first time a ROY winner also claimed the defensive prize. In Hubbs' sophomore season, the "Lovable Losers" turned their previous, dismal 59-103 record into an impressive 82-80 showing. Things were looking up for the Cubs, which, as history and championship curses have shown, is generally a temporal phenomenon. True to form, heart-wrenching tragedy stole Hubbs from his promising future the next February—a week shy of spring training—when his self-piloted private plane crashed during a flight from California to Utah. He was 22 years old. Topps soon produced this solemn tribute to "Hubbs of the Cubs," a card that still evokes strong emotion among the

IN MEMORIAM

KEN HUBBS

1964 Topps #550 "In Memoriam" — Ken Hubbs

Chicago Cubs faithful who remember that dark day in late winter of '64. *Estimated Value: $75*

I N RETROSPECT, TOPPS' DIE-cut "Stand-Ups" seem like a cruel practical joke on modern-day collectors. The 77 cards begged to be played with; that was the whole point. They were punched out and folded, yellow and pickle-green color scheme made edge wear inevitable and obvious. Twenty-two of the cards were significantly short-printed relative to their 55 counterparts, rendering Willie McCovey, Carl Yastrzemski, and

PUNCH OUT AND
BEND BACK ON
PERFORATED LINE

BOB CLEMENTE
PITTS. PIRATES   OUTFIELD

CY.C.G.   PRINTED IN U.S.A.

1964 Topps Stand-Ups — Roberto Clemente

possibly severing a limb (the ballplayer's) in the process. Depending on the buyer's origami acuity, the figure could also become detached from its surroundings or dangle by the fibers of a thigh. What's more, the full-bleed, flush-to-the-border nature of the mustard-Warren Spahn particularly difficult acquisitions. Roberto Clemente's depiction, like every "Stand-Up," bears no number, statistic, or, indeed, back-printing of any kind. The minimalist artwork ushers forth only Clemente, a nameplate, an imprinted signature, brief instructions, and a subtle perforated outline so that the Pirates idol could rise to the occasion.

Estimated Value: $495

T HE ONE-TWO PUNCH of Sandy Koufax and Don Drysdale stymied 1964's senior-circuit hitters to a per-game average of under two earned runs. Koufax's 1.74 ERA formed part of his five straight They sought 3-year contracts together worth more than $1,000,000—an unfathomable request at that time. Facing strong opposition from the Dodgers' front office, both men threatened to retire from baseball and begin

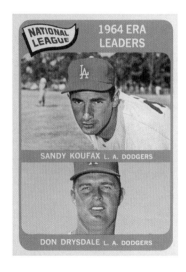

NATIONAL LEAGUE   1964 ERA LEADERS

SANDY KOUFAX L. A. DODGERS

DON DRYSDALE L. A. DODGERS

1965 Topps #8 "ERA Leaders" — Koufax/Drysdale

titles in the category from 1962 to 1966; Drysdale's 2.18 mark was the lowest of his 14-season career. The duo also fired a combined 37 wins and 460 strikeouts. In the succeeding year of this film-reel-design "Leaders" card, they set a National League record with 592 K's. Then, on February 28, 1966, Koufax and Drysdale banded together for a groundbreaking joint holdout. movie careers. They ended the holdout a month later after negotiating significant raises from their previous salaries. "Big D," who had a 1962 Cy Young Award to his credit, would bow out of baseball with a miraculous final full season in 1968—the oft-dubbed "Year of the Pitcher." He blanked the opposition in six straight shutouts for a record 58 consecutive scoreless innings. Two decades later, in a serendipitous turn of events, Drysdale's broadcasting career yielded his play-by-play call of the game when that seemingly unapproachable scoreless-innings mark was surpassed by fellow Dodger Orel Hershiser.

Estimated Value: $50

The National League All-Stars await their introductions.

BATTING LEADERS
NATIONAL LEAGUE

Player	AVG	Player	AVG
Clemente, Pitt.	.329	Fairly, L. A.	.274
H. Aaron, Mil.	.318	Stargell, Pitt.	.272
Mays, S. F.	.317	Morgan, Hou.	.271
Williams, Chi.	.315	Mazeroski, Pitt.	.271
Rose, Cin.	.312	Pagliaroni, Pitt.	.268
Flood, St. L.	.310	Banks, Chi.	.265
Pinson, Cin.	.305	Bolling, Mil.	.264
Rojas, Phil.	.303	Aspromonte, Hou.	.263
Allen, Phil.	.302	Bond, Hou.	.263
Clendenon, Pitt.	.301	Callison, Phil.	.262
Hart, S. F.	.299	Jones, Mil.	.262
J. Alou, S. F.	.298	Boyer, St. L.	.260
Alou, Mil.	.297	Johnson, L. A.	.259
Robinson, Cin.	.296	Harper, Cin.	.257
Torre, Mil.	.291	Bailey, Pitt.	.256
White, St. L.	.289	Maye, Mil.-Hou.	.256
Brock, St. L.	.288	Staub, Hou.	.256
Johnson, Cin.	.287	Groat, St. L.	.254
Cardenas, Cin.	.287	Kranepool, N. Y.	.253
Wills, L. A.	.286	Alley, Pitt.	.252
Santo, Chi.	.285	Mathews, Mil.	.251
Virdon, Pitt.	.279	Haller, S. F.	.251
McCovey, S. F.	.276	Lefebvre, L. A.	.250
McCarver, St. L.	.276	Christopher, N. Y.	.249
Wynn, Hou.	.275	Lewis, N. Y.	.245

©T.C.G. PRINTED IN U.S.A.

N. LEAGUE — **1965 BATTING LEADERS**

BOB CLEMENTE — PITTSBURGH PIRATES
HANK AARON — ATLANTA BRAVES
WILLIE MAYS — SAN FRANCISCO GIANTS

ONE OF THE ULTIMATE "Leader" cards lauds the senior circuit's top three finishers for the 1965 batting crown. Roberto Mays won Gold Glove Awards that season, and Mays also picked up MVP honors for his 52-homer onslaught. The triptych-like card's reverse delivers an exhaustive list of the National League's 50 best averages, from Clemente's pace-setting percentage all the way down to Mets outfielder Johnny Lewis'.245 mark—still well above the dreaded Mendoza Line. Topps' 215th of 598 entries in its '66 set marks the only time these three baseball immortals shared cardboard real estate.

1966 Topps #215 "Batting Leaders" — Clemente/Aaron/Mays

Clemente hit at a .329 clip, while Hank Aaron edged Willie Mays by a decimal point at .318 to .317. Both Clemente and

Estimated Value: $175

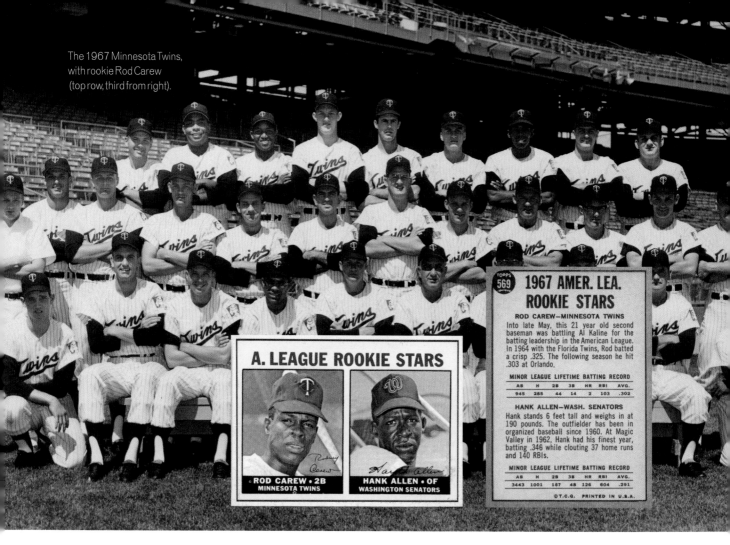

The 1967 Minnesota Twins, with rookie Rod Carew (top row, third from right).

A. LEAGUE ROOKIE STARS

- **ROD CAREW • 2B**
  MINNESOTA TWINS
- **HANK ALLEN • OF**
  WASHINGTON SENATORS

TOPPS
569

1967 AMER. LEA. ROOKIE STARS

ROD CAREW—MINNESOTA TWINS
Into late May, this 21 year old second baseman was battling Al Kaline for the batting leadership in the American League. In 1964 with the Florida Twins, Rod batted a crisp .325. The following season he hit .303 at Orlando.

MINOR LEAGUE LIFETIME BATTING RECORD

AB	H	2B	3B	HR	RBI	AVG.
945	285	44	14	2	103	.302

HANK ALLEN—WASH. SENATORS
Hank stands 6 feet tall and weighs in at 190 pounds. The outfielder has been in organized baseball since 1960. At Magic Valley in 1962, Hank had his finest year, batting .346 while clouting 37 home runs and 140 RBIs.

MINOR LEAGUE LIFETIME BATTING RECORD

AB	H	2B	3B	HR	RBI	AVG.
3443	1001	167	48	126	604	.291

©T.C.G.   PRINTED IN U.S.A.

LIKE TOM SEAVER, ROD Carew first showed up on card collectors' radar in Topps' 1967 high-number segment and then ended the season with Rookie of the Year hardware. The timing of #569's distribution allowed for a mid-season observation on the card's reverse: "Into late May, this 21 year old second baseman was battling Al Kaline for the batting leadership in the American League." Carew ultimately ranked sixth in hitting that year, but soon laid claim to a remarkable 7 of 10 batting crowns (1969, 1972-75, 1977-78). In his pinnacle year of 1977, the Panama-born speedster made a run at .400 and finished at a .388 clip. He also drove in 100 runs and crossed home plate himself 128 times. Carew's rookie-card companion, Washington Senators ballhawk Hank Allen, was a minor-league tour de force who never quite panned out in the majors. An interesting tangent on the apparently arbitrary pairing revolves around the players' respective teams. The Minnesota Twins franchise originated in 1960 with the northern migration of the Washington Senators, a move which then gave rise to the new (and not necessarily improved) second coming of the Senators from 1961 to 1971.

Estimated Value: $450

1967 TOPPS #569 "ROOKIE STARS" — ROD CAREW

The 1967 Philadelphia Phillies, with Bob Uecker (top row, fifth from right).

BACK IN 1967, THE LAST OF Bob Uecker's six big-league campaigns, anyone would have scoffed at the notion that this reserve backstop would someday be dubbed "Mr. Baseball." His career numbers amounted to what another player might consider a mediocre season—14 home runs, 74 RBI, and a .200 batting average. His claim to fame was using a tuba to shag fly balls during batting practice of the 1964 World Series. As Uecker himself once joked to a reporter, "When I looked to the third base coach for a sign, he turned his back on me." Ultimately, it was the Wisconsin native's zaniness and wit—combined with an exhaustive knowledge of the game—that made him a household name and bona-fide star of TV, film, and radio. The "Voice of the Brewers," Uecker has been broadcasting Milwaukee games since 1971, while also moonlighting on Johnny Carson's *Tonight Show*, the sitcom *Mr. Belvedere*, the *Major League* movies, and, of course, those Miller Lite commercials where he was always on the lookout for his front-row seat. Uecker also penned a light-hearted autobiography, *Catcher in the Wry*. In 2001, he was the ninth baseball announcer ever elected to the National Radio Hall of Fame, and in 2003, he won the Baseball Hall of Fame's prestigious Ford C. Frick Award for broadcasters. True to form, Uecker had the crowd in stitches during his acceptance speech at Cooperstown, at one point remarking, "I still think, and this is not sour grapes by any means, that I should have gone in as a player." *Estimated Value: $22*

1967 Topps #326 – Bob Uecker

"TOM TERRIFIC" HIT THE mound running. As a rookie, the 6-foot-1 right-hander out of USC slid right into the New York Mets starting rotation and posted the numbers of a seasoned veteran: 16 sensed which freshman hurler would bring fame to card #581. The reverse bios emphasize Denehy's credentials in the minors and Seaver's record in the bigs, making clear who had been earning his stripes so far: "*Tom won 3 out of* 1967 production is recognized as the company's last in which the high numbers are notably scarce. Naturally, their difficulty has augmented the desirability of Seaver's cardboard debut. Within a few short years of this ultra-bright col-

1967 Topps #581 "Rookie Stars" — Tom Seaver

wins, 2 shutouts, 170 strikeouts, and a 2.76 ERA. He earned All-Star and Rookie of the Year honors, proving the wisdom of the Topps braintrust in highlighting the up-and-coming ace in the '67 issue's "high-number series." True, Seaver shares space with little-known Bill Denehy, who would pitch just over 100 innings in three major-league seasons. But even so, Topps seems to have *his first 4 ballgames for the New York Mets this season. The rookie righthander clinched a job after performing sensationally in the spring exhibitions. He has only one year of minor league experience.*" Although Topps continued producing sets "in series" for the next five years (with an initial printing followed by later entries once the season had started), the 609-card lectible, Seaver would go from a dependable starter to a league standout, steering his "Amazin' Mets" to the 1969 championship on the strength of a 25-7 mark and 2.21 ERA. By career's end, he would accumulate 3,640 strikeouts, 311 victories, 12 All-Star appearances, and 3 Cy Young laurels. *Estimated Value: $750*

ALL ABOARD! "THE Ryan Express" whistled into New York to start, later tracing the rails west to California and then south to Texas over the course of a 27-year journey. Crowds gathered at every station along the way as the finely oiled machine thundered down its path at unfathomable velocity. Amazing thing was, the locomotive seemed to gain strength as the decades rolled on. Instead of breaking down and rusting like so many lesser engines, its internal fires were stoked hotter and its gears churned smoother, causing many to recite the line Roy Hobbs wished said about him in *The Natural*: "There goes the best there ever

was." Indeed, Nolan Ryan amassed spectacular credentials, the likes of which may never be repeated: 5,714 strikeouts, seven no-hitters, 12 one-hitters, and a single-season record of 383 K's in 1973. He surpassed the 300-strikeout plateau on six occasions, the last coming in 1989 at the age of 42. Ryan's arsenal of searing heat and off-speed tricks sent 1,176 different hitters skulking back to the dugout with their bats between their legs. Topps had a hunch of what was to come, dubbing the 21-year-old "one of the most promising rookies in the majors." The company's burlap-bordered issue, complete at 598 cards, pictures Ryan in a Mets hat that has yet to be broken in, his gaunt

face holding an intense, stern expression with which opposing batsmen would become all too familiar. Though he was outshined in the Big Apple by teammate Tom Seaver (and card-mate Jerry Koosman at times), the fireballer ran on all cylinders once he joined the California Angles in 1972. The Ryan Express made its final stop on September 22, 1993, and was honored for its singular track record in 1999 with enshrinement at the Hall of Fame in Cooperstown, New York—the state of its original departure. *Estimated Value: $950*

1968 Topps #177 "Rookie Stars" — Nolan Ryan

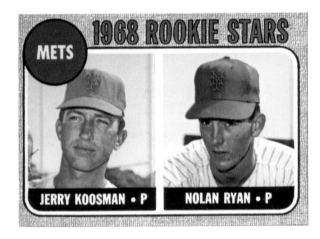

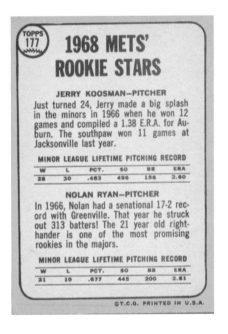

IN 1969, THE YEAR OF APOLLO 11 and Woodstock, baseball had its share of headlines. Mickey Mantle retired, the American League and National League added two new teams apiece, the Amazin'

RBI showing in 1968, Jackson exploded for what would be the best statistical campaign of his career. He clouted 47 four-baggers, drove in 118 runs, and amassed a .608 slugging percentage. (Jackson also led the league in strike-

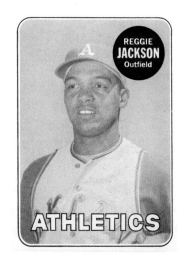

1969 TOPPS #260 – REGGIE JACKSON

Mets stole the Yankees' habitual spotlight, Ted Williams became a manager, and Oakland A's outfielder Reggie Jackson made the transition from promising rookie to second-year superstar. Jackson also scored his first cardboard cameo, appearing on the 260th of 664 entries in Topps' closing set of the sixties. His bright portrait, showcasing the Athletics' flashy uniform style, doubtless became a hotter commodity as the '69 season progressed. Fresh off a 29-homer and 74-

outs for the second of four consecutive years; he finished in the Top 10 for whiffs in every year from 1968 to 1985, and still holds the lifetime record with 2,597—a total that eclipses his career hits by 13.) Reggie made it known, loud and clear, that he had officially arrived. He would win two championships with the Athletics, then two more with the Yankees, as his intimidating, overpowering play in big games earned him the nickname "Mr. October." The brash and burly slug-

ger's finest postseason feat came in 1977, when he cleared the bases three times in a single World Series game, the first player to do so since Babe Ruth. Jackson went on to play for the California Angels in the early to mid-1980s, before completing his career in 1987 where it had begun 21 seasons earlier, with the Athletics.
Estimated Value: $475

TED WILLIAMS MADE HIS celebrated return to the majors in 1969, this time not as a feared batsman but as manager of the lowly Washington Senators. "Get a good ball

enjoyed a career year that season. He clocked 30 home runs (including three in a single game) and plated 85 runs while, defensively, committing only 11 errors. Epstein later took Ted's know-

1969 TOPPS #539 "TED SHOWS HOW" – WILLIAMS/EPSTEIN

to hit!" was his rallying cry to young hitters, and first baseman Mike Epstein certainly reaped the benefits of Williams' tutelage. A "chosen son" to many Jewish baseball fans, Epstein

how with him to the Oakland Athletics, where he led the roster with 26 round-trippers in the A's dynasty-commencing 1972 championship campaign.
Estimated Value: $40

The Mick gives his farewell speech at Yankee Stadium, June 8, 1969.

THE MICK HAD HUNG UP his pinstripes for good when Topps gave him the aptly numbered 500th slot in its closing set of the 1960s. Legions of fans who mourned Mantle's surname in yellow letters that matched "YANKEES." Others unknowingly possessed an alternate version that resulted from a color-plate error during the printing process: "MANTLE" two decades. He embodied the sport, defined it. He was an idol to millions, a staple of postseason play, a symbol of all-around athletic excellence. Topps hit a grand slam with its stirring send-

1969 TOPPS #500 WHITE-LETTER VARIATION — MICKEY MANTLE

Mantle's absence now clamored for his final career-contemporary depiction. Among those pack-buyers who found success at the corner store, most strolled home with a card that had in white. The variation has added a certain mystique to a card that, for many collectors of a certain age and sentiment, evokes a wave of emotion. Mickey Mantle *was* baseball for almost off to Mantle and to the halcyon era defined by him.
Estimated Value: $5,500

OVER THE PAST FEW decades, many sports collectible areas have come into their own both from the standpoints of popularity and value—but baseball cards continue to reign supreme.

a proven investment with an exceptional return.

As a case in point, I recently selected a bundle of 100 different mainstream sports cards and tracked them over an 11-year period of time since the inception of PSA and of price-tracking graded cards (see Table). In 1995, this group of cards would have cost you $986,875 in investor-grade Near Mint to Mint condition. Today, however, this

perform and out-perform the overall market; but, overall, high-grade sports cards are a solid investment.

What does this all mean? With the consistency offered by respected independent card-grading services, along-

APPENDIX A: BASEBALL CARDS AS AN INVESTMENT...NO LONGER SIMPLY CHILD'S PLAY — DOUG ALLEN

Simply stated, demand continues to exceed supply when it comes to rare and/or high-grade examples, and as a result their values never cease to escalate at a rapid pace. The emergence of

side the depth of an established market that has demonstrated reliably strong performance over the last decade, you could safely put together an investment portfolio of mainstream sports cards

professionally and independently graded cards by companies such as Professional Sports Authenticator (PSA) has contributed to the view of sports cards as an asset class in and of themselves. Yes, collectors can indeed tell their significant others that the purchases feeding their passion are in fact

same group of cards would cost you $2,401,940. This return of 143% compares favorably to both the S&P 500 and the Dow Jones Industrial, which showed a return over the same period of 153% and 133%, respectively. Similar to the stock market, anomalies exist where certain cards both under-

that we are confident will perform well. And, armed with the baseball-card history and values presented in this book, you will be able to do just that.

Doug Allen, President
Mastro Auctions

NO.	CARD YEAR/ISSUE	CARD NO.	PLAYER	April 1995 NM-MT 8	April 2006 NR-MT 8
1	1911 T205		COBB	$6750	$72500
2	1911 T205		JOHNSON	2600	20000
3	1911 T205		MATHEWSON	1900	17500
4	1911 T205		YOUNG	2100	16500
5	1911 T205		COBB (RED PORTRAIT)	4000	12500
6	1909–1911 T206		JOHNSON (PORTRAIT)	2000	13000
7	1909–1911 T206		MATHEWSON (PORTRAIT)	1775	13500
8	1909–1911 T206		MAGIE (ERROR)	35500	55000
9	1909–1911 T206		PLANK	52500	225000
10	1909–1911 T206		WAGNER	430000	1265000
11	1915 CRACKER JACK	30	COBB	12500	25000
12	1915 CRACKER JACK	57	JOHNSON	4500	12500
13	1915 CRACKER JACK	88	MATHEWSON	3500	12500
14	1915 CRACKER JACK	103	JACKSON	15000	35000
15	1933 GOUDEY	1	BENGOUGH	7800	15000
16	1933 GOUDEY	53	RUTH	12000	42500
17	1933 GOUDEY	92	GEHRIG	4500	8750
18	1933 GOUDEY	106	LAJOIE	62500	50000
19	1933 GOUDEY	144	RUTH	8000	18500
20	1933 GOUDEY	149	RUTH	8000	32500
21	1933 GOUDEY	160	GEHRIG	4500	14000
22	1933 GOUDEY	181	RUTH	8000	18000
23	1933 SPORT KINGS	1	COBB	3750	12500
24	1933 SPORT KINGS	2	RUTH	6500	27500
25	1934 GOUDEY	37	GEHRIG	4850	11500
26	1934 GOUDEY	61	GEHRIG	4850	9750
27	1938 GOUDEY	250	DIMAGGIO	5250	8500
28	1938 GOUDEY	274	DIMAGGIO	5500	9750

NO.	CARD YEAR/ISSUE	CARD NO.	PLAYER	April 1995 NM-MT 8	April 2006 NR-MT 8
29	1939 PLAY BALL	26	DIMAGGIO	2300	3250
30	1939 PLAY BALL	92	WILLIAMS	3250	5500
31	1940 PLAY BALL	1	DIMAGGIO	3250	12000
32	1940 PLAY BALL	27	WILLIAMS	2600	5250
33	1940 PLAY BALL	225	JACKSON	3500	7500
34	1941 PLAY BALL	14	WILLIAMS	3750	5500
35	1941 PLAY BALL	71	DIMAGGIO	4250	11000
36	1949 LEAF	1	DIMAGGIO	5750	12500
37	1949 LEAF	3	RUTH	5750	6500
38	1949 LEAF	8	PAIGE	4750	42500
39	1949 LEAF	76	WILLIAMS	2000	6000
40	1949 LEAF	79	ROBINSON	2000	8500
41	1949 LEAF	93	FELLER	3250	11500
42	1949 BOWMAN	24	MUSIAL	1400	1200
43	1949 BOWMAN	50	ROBINSON	2000	2800
44	1949 BOWMAN	84	CAMPANELLA	1750	1100
45	1949 BOWMAN	224	PAIGE	2700	2700
46	1949 BOWMAN	226	SNIDER	2600	2000
47	1950 BOWMAN	22	ROBINSON	2000	3000
48	1950 BOWMAN	98	WILLIAMS	2100	2500
49	1951 BOWMAN	1	FORD	2750	7250
50	1951 BOWMAN	165	WILLIAMS	2000	2300
51	1951 BOWMAN	253	MANTLE	25000	16500
52	1951 BOWMAN	305	MAYS	8750	9000
53	1952 BOWMAN	1	BERRA	1500	2900
54	1952 BOWMAN	101	MANTLE	5250	3400
55	1952 BOWMAN	218	MAYS	2900	3200
56	1952 TOPPS	1	PAFKO	10500	15000
57	1952 TOPPS	261	MAYS	6000	6250
58	1952 TOPPS	311	MANTLE	45000	54000+
59	1952 TOPPS	312	ROBINSON	3750	3500
60	1952 TOPPS	407	MATHEWS	8500	20000

NO.	CARD YEAR/ISSUE	CARD NO.	PLAYER	April 1995 NM-MT 8	April 2006 NR-MT 8
61	1953 BOWMAN COLOR	33	REESE	2000	1500
62	1953 BOWMAN COLOR	59	MANTLE	4500	3250
63	1953 TOPPS	1	ROBINSON	2100	2600
64	1953 TOPPS	82	MANTLE	8000	7000
65	1953 TOPPS	244	MAYS	7500	7500
66	1954 BOWMAN	66	WILLIAMS	8000	6250
67	1954 TOPPS	1	WILLIAMS	1500	3750
68	1954 TOPPS	90	MAYS	1400	1300
69	1954 TOPPS	94	BANKS	2025	2200
70	1954 TOPPS	128	AARON	4500	3000
71	1954 TOPPS	201	KALINE	1700	1000
72	1954 TOPPS	250	WILLIAMS	1700	3250
73	1955 TOPPS	123	KOUFAX	2100	1850
74	1955 TOPPS	164	CLEMENTE	5000	4600
75	1956 TOPPS	135	MANTLE	3100	2500
76	1957 TOPPS	1	WILLIAMS	1400	1500
77	1957 TOPPS	35	ROBINSON	600	750
78	1957 TOPPS	95	MANTLE	2500	2200
79	1957 TOPPS	328	ROBINSON	800	650
80	1958 TOPPS	1	WILLIAMS	1100	1850
81	1958 TOPPS	30	AARON (YL)	1050	750
82	1958 TOPPS	52	CLEMENTE (YL)	1100	2750
83	1958 TOPPS	150	MANTLE	1700	2500
84	1959 TOPPS	10	MANTLE	1250	2300
85	1959 TOPPS	564	MANTLE	600	610
86	1960 TOPPS	350	MANTLE	1100	1100
87	1961 TOPPS	300	MANTLE	950	950
88	1962 TOPPS	200	MANTLE	1250	1650
89	1963 TOPPS	200	MANTLE	1000	1150

NO.	CARD YEAR/ISSUE	CARD NO.	PLAYER	April 1995 NM-MT 8	April 2006 NR-MT 8
90	1963 TOPPS	537	ROSE	1900	1650
91	1964 TOPPS	50	MANTLE	675	750
92	1965 TOPPS	350	MANTLE	125	900
93	1966 TOPPS	1	MAYS	350	850
94	1966 TOPPS	50	MANTLE	550	525
95	1967 TOPPS	150	MANTLE	625	550
96	1967 TOPPS	581	SEAVER	1650	750
97	1968 TOPPS	177	RYAN	2900	950
98	1968 TOPPS	280	MANTLE	550	430
99	1969 TOPPS	260	JACKSON	800	475
100	1969 TOPPS	500	MANTLE(WL)	1750	5500
Grand Total				$986,875	$2,401,940
% Increase					143%
S&P 500				$475	$1,200
% Increase					153%
Dow Jones Ind.				$4,500	$10,500
% Increase					133%

IT IS AN EXCITING DAY TO BE a card collector—perhaps more exciting than any other time in hobby history. Never before have so many great collectibles been available to the consumer, courtesy of the sellers, who naturally had a financial interest in their inventory, became the authenticator and grader by default. They determined whether an item was genuine, evaluated the technical grade, and then sold the item to a buyer under those pretenses. The inherent bias was unavoidable. Without universally attempted to provide a solution to some of these major problems associated with the buying and selling of cards. Third-party grading was a radical and controversial concept at the time. Slowly but surely, though, and with the

APPENDIX B: THE GRADING REVOLUTION — JOE ORLANDO

Internet and high-end sellers like Mastro Auctions. Never before have passionate collectors been privy to so many educational resources about cards, thanks to Web sites and publications such as this informative book. Never before have consumers felt as much peace of mind and confidence as they do in our current age of credible third-party authentication and grading.

Twenty years ago, during the hobby boom of the 1980s, there were two major issues plaguing the card industry: 1) conflict of interest and 2) the lack of an accepted grading standard. Card accepted standards, dealers and collectors relied on their own subjective interpretations. What was "Mint" to one person was only "Near Mint" to another. Sometimes, a consumer would purchase a card in one condition, only to have the grade reduced to another condition when it came time to sell the card—even if selling it back to the very same dealer!

Enter third-party grading.

In 1991, a little company called PSA (Professional Sports Authenticator) help of a small yet influential group of market leaders, consumers realized the importance of third-party grading and eventually insisted on the service. This growing standardization brought stability and collector confidence back to the marketplace. The card industry was changed forever.

Demand for graded cards has increased with every passing year. Up until 1998, the year of the great home run duel between Mark McGwire and Sammy Sosa, PSA had received 1,000,000 graded-card submissions. In the subsequent 8 years, from 1999

to 2006, we have graded approximately 9,000,000 more cards—averaging over 1,000,000 per year. After 10,000,000-plus card submissions in our 15-year history, it's safe to say that the concept of third-party grading is

lectibles such as autographs, game-used bats and photos, but it is that early experience with baseball cards that connects virtually all of us. The baseball card is a symbol of how it all started.

As someone who has thoroughly

lectors an opportunity to meet people who can help maximize their experience and provide the type of positive recognition that most hobbyists crave.

When you consider where card collecting has been and where it is going,

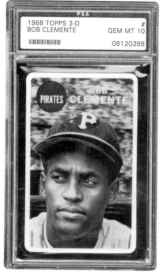

here to stay.

Baseball cards have been the backbone of this hobby since the beginning. They provide a link to our history, both on a personal and social level. These tiny time capsules remind us of where we came from and how things have changed in our great nation's history. From baseball's beginnings to the era of the Bambino, from Jackie Robinson breaking the color barrier to Cal Ripken becoming baseball's Iron Man, each card tells a story. How some of these fragile pieces of cardboard have survived the test of time is a story in itself. Baseball cards bring us back to our youth, helping us relive the experience of opening packs, trading with our friends and following our heroes religiously on the field. Over time, some collectors branch out into other col-

enjoyed this hobby throughout his entire life, I would like to share a suggestion of how to enhance your collecting experience: Learn as much as you possibly can, not only about the cards you want to buy, but also about the authentication and grading services you may choose to use. Not all third-party services carry the same level of respect and brand strength. Ask questions of those people you trust—reputable dealers, auction houses and fellow hobbyists. An educated collector is a happy collector, and there are more resources available today than ever before. The hobby is a community filled with people who share the same passion that drives you to build upon your collection. Programs such as the PSA Set Registry and events like the National Sports Collectibles Convention give col-

the future offers exciting possibilities. With each passing year, the industry matures, evolves and thrives for the betterment of all its participants. The grading revolution has played a vital role in the hobby's market expansion.

Enjoy this wonderful book and happy collecting!

Joe Orlando
President of Professional Sports Authenticator (PSA) and PSA/DNA Authentication Services, and editor of Sports Market Report (SMR)

Over the next several pages, you will see a guide to the PSA grading standard. Various images of the legendary 1952 Topps Mickey Mantle card will provide a visual reference for each grading tier, as well as illustrate the variances within each grade. Our professional graders analyze the strength of characteristics such as corners, centering, color, clarity and print quality, while also considering flaws like toning, staining, print defects, creasing and general wear. One additional factor can be difficult to scientifically measure, but remains critical: eye appeal. The eye-appeal factor may be the difference between an average PSA NM 7 and an exceptional one, or between a high-end PSA NM 7 versus a PSA NM-MT 8. I hope that this guide provides you with a thorough understanding of our grading approach.

Joe Orlando

PSA Card Grading Standards

GEM-MT 10: Gem Mint

A PSA Gem Mint 10 card is a virtually perfect card. Attributes include four perfectly sharp corners, sharp focus and full original gloss. A PSA Gem Mint 10 card must be free of staining of any kind, but an allowance may be made for a slight printing imperfection, if it doesn't impair the overall appeal of the card. The image must be centered on the card within a tolerance not to exceed approximately 55/45 to 60/40 percent on the front, and 75/25 percent on the reverse.

MINT 9: Mint

A PSA Mint 9 is a superb condition card that exhibits only one of the following minor flaws: a very slight wax stain on reverse, a minor printing imperfection or slightly off-white borders. Centering must be approximately 60/40 to 65/35 or better on the front and 90/10 or better on the reverse.

NM-MT 8: Near Mint-Mint

A PSA NM-MT 8 is a super high-end card that appears Mint 9 at first glance, but upon closer inspection, the card can exhibit the following: a very slight wax stain on reverse, slightest fraying at one or two corners, a minor printing imperfection, and/or slightly off-white borders. Centering must be approximately 65/35 to 70/30 or better on the front and 90/10 or better on the reverse.

NM 7: Near Mint

A PSA NM 7 is a card with just a slight surface wear visible upon close inspection. There may be slight fraying on some corners. Picture focus may be slightly out-of-register. A minor printing blemish is acceptable. Slight wax staining is acceptable on the back of the card only. Most of the original gloss is retained. Centering must be approximately 70/30 to 75/25 or better on the front and 90/10 or better on the back.

EX-MT 6: Excellent-Mint

A PSA EX-MT 6 card may have visible surface wear or a printing defect which does not detract from its overall appeal. A very light scratch may be detected only upon close inspection. Corners may have slightly graduated fraying. Picture focus may be slightly out-of-register. Card may show some loss of original gloss, may have minor wax stain on reverse, may exhibit very slight notching on edges and may also show some off-whiteness on borders. Centering must be 80/20 or better on the front and 90/10 or better on the reverse.

EX 5: Excellent

On PSA EX-5 cards, very minor rounding of the corners is becoming evident. Surface wear or printing defects are more visible. There may be minor chipping on edges. Loss of original gloss will be more apparent. Focus of picture may be slightly out-of-register. Several light scratches may be visible upon close inspection, but do not detract from the appeal of the card. Card may show some off-whiteness of borders. Centering must be 85/15 or better on the front and 90/10 or better on the back.

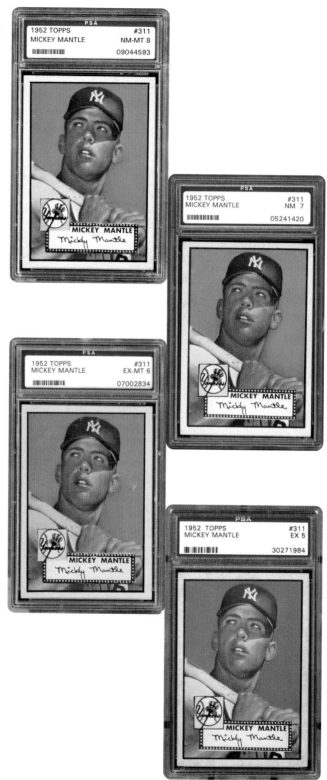

VG-EX 4: Very Good-Excellent

A PSA VG-EX 4 card's corners may be slightly rounded. Surface wear is noticeable but modest. The card may have light scuffing or light scratches. Some original gloss will be retained. Borders may be slightly off-white. A light crease may be visible. Centering must be 85/15 or better on the front and 90/10 or better on the back.

VG 3: Very Good

A PSA VG 3 card reveals some rounding of the corners, though not extreme. Some surface wear will be apparent, along with possible light scuffing or light scratches. Focus may be somewhat off-register and edges may exhibit noticeable wear. Much, but not all, of the card's original gloss will be lost. Borders may be somewhat yellowed and/or discolored. A crease may be visible. Printing defects are possible. Slight stain may show on obverse and wax staining on reverse may be more prominent. Centering must be 90/10 or better on the front and back.

GOOD 2: Good

A PSA Good 2 card's corners show accelerated rounding and surface wear is starting to become obvious. A good card may have scratching, scuffing, light staining, or chipping of enamel on obverse. There may be several creases. Original gloss may be completely absent. Card may show considerable discoloration. Centering must be 90/10 or better on the front and back.

PR-FR 1: Poor to Fair

A PSA PR-FR 1 card's corners will show extreme wear, possibly affecting framing of picture. Surface of card will show advanced stages of wear, including scuffing, scratching, pitting, chipping and staining. Picture will possibly be quite out-of-register and borders may have become brown and dirty. May have one or more heavy creases. A Poor card may be missing one or more small pieces, have major creasing and extreme discoloration or dirtiness throughout. Card may show noticeable warping. Centering must be 90/10 or better on the front and back.

INDEX

ABOUT THE AUTHORS

KHYBER GREW UP IN the hobby. He spent countless hours hanging around his dad's card stores, tagging along at shows, getting to know dealers, hunting for Mark McGwire and Cal Ripken Jr. rookies, and memorizing career-leader lists out of *The Baseball Encyclopedia*. In college at Penn State, Khyber focused his attention on writing and social work. He majored in English and wrote a senior thesis titled *Healing Through Group Writing: A Workshop Manual for Counselors of Women Survivors of Sexual Violence* (available at www.pcar.org). Khyber has been a copywriter with Mastro Auctions' Sports and Americana divisions for the past four years. He recently co-authored the company's guidebook, *A Portrait of Baseball Photography: The Definitive History of our Pastime's Pictures, News Services and Photographers.*

Acknowledgements

My thanks go first to Mark, for producing and funding this project, and to my dad Ron, for editing the book's content and card choices. I've been grateful for the opportunity to work alongside both of you over the past year as we bridged the geographic gap with constant emails between Aspen, Columbus, and Philadelphia.

This book would not have been possible without the help of Mastro Auctions' head writer Brian Bigelow

KHYBER OSER

Photo by Ethan Colchamiro

and hobby stalwart Jim Johnston, both of whose wide-ranging card knowledge was an asset to me and shows up throughout these pages; as well as Mastro Auctions' IT director Bill Boehm, whose ingenious database system made it possible to reference six years' worth of previous catalog descriptions and images.

I would also like to thank several other members of the Mastro Auctions family: Doug Allen, president and COO,

for seeing the value in this book and deciding to publish it; Jeff Marren, creative director, for going above and beyond the call of duty, as always, by contributing to the project's vision in many more ways than simply the fantastic layout; Kevin Struss, vintage card specialist, for his critical guidance and expertise in the later stages of editing; Scott Emmerling, graphic/web designer, and Sarah Kraft, administrative assistant, for locating and retrieving the archived images, and for Sarah's work on marketing the book; Pete Calderon, vintage card writer, for his superb candy-card suggestions; Tim Frystak, writer and researcher, for being kind enough to proofread the text; and Bill Mastro, chairman and CEO, for his valuable input.

I'm grateful to my wife Maren, who somehow always finds the time to read my writing from cover to cover and lend me her expert editorial advice, no matter how much work she has on her own plate or how much baseball lingo she has to wade through.

Lastly, I would like to make a special dedication of this book to my grandmother, Frances Kaufman, who, at 86, remains a constant source of inspiration and wisdom to me.

*F*RIEDLAND GRADUATED from Northwestern University (1979) and the University of Miami Law School (1982), where he was selected to the Law Review. Today, he operates several business enter-prises from his office in Aspen, Colorado, including New Age Beverage Distribution, Pure Water Factory, Whirling Logos Advertising, Aspen Fiber Optics and Genesis Networks. Friedland has amassed a variety of collections over the years, focusing primarily on presidential and campaign documents and textiles, as well as signed and unsigned baseball cards. He co-hosts a local public television show known as *The Quills of History*, which addresses various topics of historical interest. Like Navin Johnson, Friedland is most proud of the fact that his name appears in the local phone directory.

Acknowledgements

John Donne correctly stated, "No man is an island, entire of itself." I am

MARK FRIEDLAND

assistant Beth Donahue, who manages my insane existence and whose insight and suggestions can be found throughout the text. To Millard and Susan Zimet for their wisdom and wit. To Don Drapkin for his counsel and advice in all walks of life. To Dan Carney for staying

indebted to many individuals, present and past, in conceptualizing this book. To Ron and Khyber Oser for transforming an idea into reality. To Doug Allen for assuring that reality. To Mike Campbell, the expert's expert. To my friend and the course. To Chris Tolk for testing my intellectual mettle while slurping Vietnamese noodle soup. To Jerry Bovino for being there. To Matt Avril for being Matt Avril. To the following friends who represent the many whom I am remiss in not mentioning: Raifie Bass, Jordan Bittel, Steven Bittel, Rob Borden, Norman Braman, Bobby Ferguson, Allan Friedland, Larry Golinksy, Laurie Holtz, Howard Scharlin, Larry Slabotsky and Skip Strasbourger. To our parents and role models, Joel and Paula Friedland and Tom and Sally Fleming. To my adorable sisters Robin and Vicki, and to our four children, Michael, Sean, Jordan and Carson, a constant source of pride and joy. To my wife Hunter, my muse, my inspiration, my North Star. Finally, to my childhood card-flipping buddies at Camp Blue Star and Camp Akiba, especially Stephen Euster, whose memory will never be forgotten.

A RESPECTED FIGURE in the hobby, Ron has been dealing in pre-war baseball cards and vintage non-sports issues for more than 25 years. He made his name with retail comic book/baseball card stores, spent many years on the road at weekend conventions, and later formed the auction business Ron Oser Enterprises. Landing with Mastro Auctions six years ago, Ron is currently a company vice-president and runs the day-to-day operations of the East Coast office. He also travels frequently to gather consignments for the firm's three divisions—Sports, Americana and Fine Art—and takes great pleasure in the treasure-hunt aspect of his job. Ron's mantra about his long career in collectibles is a simple one: "It sure beats working!"

Acknowledgements

To my good friend Mark Friedland, the architect for this project's overall

RON OSER

concept and the driving force for all of us involved in bringing it to fruition.

To my son Khyber, whose intelligence, intuition and inherent compassion are a never-ending source of pride and joy.

To my Mastro Auctions compatriots Doug Allen, Bill Mastro, Jeff Marren, Brian Bigelow, Bill Boehm and many others, whose invaluable input and tireless work ethic have been instrumental in the creation of this book.

To the rest of my family, my son Bodhi and daughters Amber and Autumn, who are the lights of my life, and most importantly to my wonderful wife Janet, who gives my life love and meaning beyond words.